John Mitchel

JAMES QUINN

Published on behalf of the
Historical Association of Ireland
by

UNIVERSITY COLLEGE DUBLIN PRESS
PREAS CHOLÁISTE OLLSCOILE
BHAILE ÁTHA CLIATH

2008

First published 2008 on behalf of the
Historical Association of Ireland
by University College Dublin Press

© James Quinn 2008

ISBN 978–1–906359–15–7
ISSN 2009–1397

University College Dublin Press
Newman House, 86 St Stephen's Green
Dublin 2, Ireland
www.ucdpress.ie

CIP data available from the British Library

*The right of James Quinn to be identified as
the author of this work has been asserted by him*

Typeset in Bantry, Ireland in Ehrhardt by Elaine Burberry
Text design by Lyn Davies
Printed in England on acid-free paper by
MPG Books, Bodmin, Cornwall

CONTENTS

FOREWORD

Originally conceived over a decade ago to place the lives of leading figures in Irish history against the background of new research on the problems and conditions of their times and modern assessments of their historical significance, the Historical Association of Ireland Life and Times series enjoyed remarkable popularity and success. A second series has now been planned in association with UCD Press in a new format and with fuller scholarly apparatus. Encouraged by the reception given to the earlier series, the volumes in the new series will be expressly designed to be of particular help to students preparing for the Leaving Certificate, for GCE Advanced Level and for undergraduate history courses as well as appealing to the happily insatiable appetite for new views of Irish history among the general public.

CIARAN BRADY
Historical Association of Ireland

PREFACE

Several people helped me with the preparation of this book. My colleagues on the Royal Irish Academy's *Dictionary of Irish Biography*, James McGuire, Lawrence White and Patrick Maume, were kind enough to read the first draft, and all three made valuable suggestions. I am grateful to them and very fortunate to have benefited from the knowledge and experience of such excellent historians. I also wish to thank all my other colleagues on the *Dictionary* for their support, and to thank the staff of the library of the Royal Irish Academy for their invaluable help. Patrick Geoghegan of Trinity College Dublin kindly brought to my attention some American sources which otherwise I would have missed.

I am grateful to Ciaran Brady for giving me the opportunity to write this work, and also for his general encouragement and historical insights. I also wish to thank Colm Croker for his meticulous copy-editing.

JAMES QUINN
Dictionary of Irish Biography
Royal Irish Academy

CHRONOLOGY OF MITCHEL'S LIFE AND TIMES

1815
18 June Napoleon defeated at Waterloo (abdicates 22 June).
3 November John Mitchel born near Dungiven, County Derry.

1821
August–October serious failure of potato crop.

1822
June–December fever and famine in the west of Ireland.

1823
12 May Daniel O'Connell founds the Catholic Association.
Mitchel family moves to Dromalane, near Newry, County Down.

1824
24 January O'Connell initiates 'Catholic rent' by collecting a penny a month from associate members of the Catholic Association.
Catholic emancipation becomes a truly popular cause.

1828
5 July O'Connell elected MP for County Clare.

1829
13 April Catholic Relief Act (1829) enables Catholics to enter parliament and hold high civil and military office.

1830
27–29 July revolution in Paris overthrows Charles X.
9 August Louis-Philippe accepts throne.
25 August revolution in Belgium against union with the Dutch.
18 November Belgium declares independence.

1831

25 January Polish diet declares independence of Poland; brutally suppressed by Russian troops (May).

4 July Mitchel enters TCD.

1832

7 June Reform Act gives the vote to middle classes and abolishes many small boroughs.

1834

22–30 April O'Connell proposes repeal of union in House of Commons; defeated 523 to 38.

1835

January Whigs win narrow victory in general election.

18 February Lichfield House conference: O'Connell agrees to abandon agitation for repeal of the Act of Union and to support the Whigs in return for liberal reforms in Ireland.

1836

16 February Mitchel graduates BA (TCD).

1837

2 February Mitchel and Jane (Jenny) Verner elope and marry.

1838

31 July Poor Relief Act extends new English poor law of 1834 to Ireland; elected boards of guardians set up to administer a workhouse system; poor rate to be levied on landlords and tenants.

15 August Tithe Act converts tithe to rent charge and scales down amount payable; removes tithe as a popular grievance.

1840

February John Mitchel senior dies.

15 April O'Connell founds Repeal Association to renew agitation for repeal.

August Archbishop John MacHale of Tuam joins the Repeal Association, followed by many bishops and parochial clergy.

1841

17 April Thomas Davis joins the Repeal Association.

July general election – overwhelming Tory victory; only 20 repealers elected.

1842

22–23 February first National Repeal Convention of America meets in Philadelphia and splits on the abolition of slavery.

15 October first issue of the *Nation*, edited by Charles Gavan Duffy, assisted by Thomas Davis and John Blake Dillon.

1843

January O'Connell announces 1843 will be 'Repeal year', and holds monster meetings at Trim (9 March), Mallow (11 June) and the Hill of Tara (15 August).

May Mitchel joins the Repeal Association.

7 October proclamation prohibits repeal meeting at Clontarf; O'Connell cancels meeting. 20 October: William Smith O'Brien joins the Repeal Association.

20 November Devon Commission appointed to inquire into Irish land system; reports in February 1845 recommending compensation to tenants for improvements.

1844

10 February O'Connell and eight others found guilty of conspiracy.

30 May sentenced to twelve months' imprisonment.

4 September House of Lords reverses judgement against O'Connell and others, who are all released.

1845

12, 26 May O'Connell and Davis differ over Irish Colleges Bill at Repeal Association meetings.

9 September potato blight arrives in Ireland.

16 September Davis dies aged 30.

September Mitchel's *Life of Aodh O'Neill* published.

9 October Mitchel becomes assistant editor of the *Nation* and moves to Dublin.

1846

26 June corn laws repealed (duties on imported corn and grain abolished); Tories split and (30 June) Lord John Russell (Whig) replaces Peel as prime minister (until 23 February 1852).

28 July Young Irelanders split from Repeal Association after debates on physical force.

July–August disastrous failure of potato crop.

1847

11 January James Fintan Lalor writes private letter to Duffy advocating agrarian reform and Irish independence to be achieved by a rent strike.

13 January Irish Confederation formed at Rotunda, Dublin; Mitchel elected to its policy council.

15 May O'Connell dies at Genoa.

May Ulster Tenant Right Association formed in Derry.

19 September meeting of tenant farmers at Holycross, County Tipperary, convened by Lalor to form tenant league.

9 December Mitchel resigns from the *Nation* over differences with Duffy.

1848

2–4 February Irish Confederation adopts constitutional policy of O'Brien and Duffy and rejects Mitchel's call for rent and rate strike.

12 February first issue of Mitchel's *United Irishman*.

22–24 February revolution in Paris; Louis-Philippe abdicates and a republic proclaimed.

27 February national workshops established in Paris on Louis Blanc's plan to provide relief for workers.

March–April revolution spreads across Europe.

3 April in Paris O'Brien and Meagher present a fraternal address from the Irish Confederation to the French Republic.

22 April Treason-Felony Act introduces severe penalties for sedition.

26–27 May Mitchel convicted under Treason-Felony Act; sentenced to 14 years' transportation; last issue of the *United Irishman*.

1 June Mitchel sails for imprisonment in Bermuda.

23–24 June 'June days' in Paris; insurrection by Paris workers after closing of National Workshops crushed by French government; thousands killed.

8 July Duffy arrested.

25 July habeas corpus suspended until March 1849.

29 July O'Brien and 100 supporters engage 40 police at Ballingarry, County Tipperary; their efforts quickly fizzle out.

5 August O'Brien arrested.

7–23 October O'Brien, Meagher, T. B. McManus and Patrick O'Donohoe sentenced to death for treason.

10 December Louis Napoleon elected president of the French Republic.

1849

9 February Rome proclaimed a republic under Giuseppe Mazzini.

3 July French army occupy Rome and restore Pope Pius IX (12 April 1850).

22 April Mitchel transferred to Cape of Good Hope for health reasons.

5 June sentences of O'Brien and others commuted to transportation for life.

9 July O'Brien and others sent to Van Diemen's Land.

19 September Mitchel arrives at Cape, but local inhabitants refuse to accept convicts.

1850

7 April Mitchel arrives at Van Diemen's Land.

9 August Irish Tenant League founded in Dublin to seek tenant right.

1851

18 June Mitchel's family arrives at Van Diemen's Land.

2 December coup d'état of Louis Napoleon.

1852

2 December Louis Napoleon proclaimed Emperor Napoleon III.

1853

19 July Mitchel escapes from Van Diemen's Land.

9 October Mitchel arrives in San Francisco.

29 November Mitchel arrives in New York.

1854

7 January first issue of Mitchel's *Citizen* (New York).

14 January first instalment of Mitchel's 'Jail Journal' in the *Citizen* (to 19 August); published in book form (New York, 1854).

28 March Britain declares war on Russia; outbreak of Crimean War (ends 16 January 1856).

13 April Irishmen's Civil and Military Republican Union founded in New York; Mitchel a leading founder.

30 May Kansas–Nebraska Act repeals Missouri Compromise of 1820: slavery issue to be decided by popular sovereignty, leading to serious clashes between pro- and anti-slavery elements in Kansas.

December Mitchel resigns from the *Citizen*.

1855

March Mitchel moves to Knoxville, east Tennessee, and thence to a farm at Tucaleechee Cove.

1856

September Mitchel returns to Knoxville.

1857

10 May Indian army revolts against British rule (ends July 1858).

October first issue of the *Southern Citizen*, edited by Mitchel.

1858

17 March secret society later known as IRB founded in Dublin by James Stephens.

December Mitchel moves the *Southern Citizen* to Washington, DC.

1859

April Fenian Brotherhood founded in USA by John O'Mahony.

27 April France, allied with Piedmont, declares war on Austria.

August Mitchel goes to Paris.

1860

February Mitchel returns to Washington.

11 May Garibaldi invades Sicily–Naples (enters Naples 7 September).

September Mitchel returns to Paris.

6 November Abraham Lincoln (Republican) wins US presidential
election.

1861
4 February six southern states elect Jefferson Davis as president of
Confederate States of America (five more states join April–May).

17 March Victor Emmanuel II of Piedmont–Sardinia becomes king of
Italy.

12 April American Civil War begins.

1862
September–October Mitchel returns to America to support Confederacy
and becomes editor of the *Richmond Enquirer*.

22 September Lincoln declares all slaves emancipated from 1 January 1863.

1863
1–3 July major defeat for Confederacy at Gettysburg; William (Mitchel's
youngest son) killed in battle.

December Mitchel quits the *Enquirer* to write for the *Richmond Examiner*.

1864
21 January Irish National League (to restore an independent Irish
parliament) founded by John Martin and The O'Donoghue.

7 March Archbishop Paul Cullen issues St Patrick's Day pastoral
denouncing Fenianism.

20 July John (Mitchel's eldest son) killed at Fort Sumter.

1865
3 April Union army takes the Confederate capital, Richmond.

26 April American Civil War ends.

14 June Mitchel arrested by Federal government in New York (imprisoned
until 30 October).

10 November Mitchel sails for France to become financial agent for the
Fenians.

1866
March–May Fenian attacks on Canada.
22 June Mitchel resigns as Fenian agent.
August Prussia defeats Austria and annexes several German states.
October Mitchel returns to Richmond.

1867
5–6 March outbreak of Fenian rebellion around Dublin and in Munster.
18 September Manchester rescue.
October first issue of Mitchel's *Irish Citizen* (to July 1872).
23 November 'Manchester martyrs' executed at Salford.
13 December Fenian bomb at Clerkenwell prison kills 12 and injures hundreds.

1868
22 February–24 April Mitchel denounces Fenianism in the *Irish Citizen*.
November Amnesty Association founded in Dublin to seek release of Fenian prisoners.
3 December Gladstone becomes prime minister (to 20 February 1874).

1869
26 July legislation enacting disestablishment of Church of Ireland (comes into force 1 January 1871).

1870
19 May Home Government Association founded by Isaac Butt in Dublin.
19 July France declares war on Prussia; after a series of French defeats a republic is declared in Paris (4 September).
1 August Land Act gives legal protection to Ulster custom.

1871
17 January John Martin elected MP for County Meath in first victory of the Home Government Association.
18 January William I of Prussia proclaimed German emperor at Versailles.
18 March rising of Paris Commune (defeated 28 May).

1872

18 July Ballot Act institutes secret voting.

1874

February Conservatives win general election; Mitchel fails to win seat in Cork city.

3 March Home Rulers win 60 seats and constitute themselves a separate and distinct party.

July–September Mitchel visits Ireland.

30 July Joseph Biggar and others use obstruction in House of Commons despite criticisms from Butt.

1875

16 February Mitchel elected MP for County Tipperary.

17 February arrives in Ireland.

18 February declared ineligible.

12 March re-elected.

20 March Mitchel dies at his childhood home in Dromalane, County Down.

29 March John Martin dies; his County Meath seat won by Charles Stewart Parnell (19 April).

26 May Mitchel having again been declared ineligible, his seat is assigned to the Conservative runner-up.

ABBREVIATIONS

HO	Home Office (London)
IRB	Irish Republican Brotherhood
MP	Member of Parliament
NAI	National Archives of Ireland
NLI	National Library of Ireland
PRO	Public Record Office (London)
PRONI	Public Record Office of Northern Ireland
RIA	Royal Irish Academy
TCD	Trinity College Dublin
TNA	The National Archives, Kew

Introduction

What William Butler Yeats termed 'the rancorous, devil-possessed' writings of John Mitchel strike an unpleasant and disturbing note for many readers. The beliefs of no other influential Irish nationalist seem so fired with intolerance and hatred. For many modern historians he represents the unacceptable face of Irish nationalism, a bitter zealot who hated England much more than he loved Ireland: Tom Garvin describes him as 'a profoundly unattractive figure'; Roy Foster notes his 'almost psychotic Anglophobia' and R. V. Comerford his 'glorification of hatred'; while for Malcolm Brown, Mitchel's *Jail Journal* is a 'sustained nausea'.[1]

Mitchel's bitter anglophobe invective still has the power to shock 150 years after it was written. He is also notorious for his vehement support for slavery in America, a position that left him open to the charge that his conception of liberty was a narrow and selfish one. He had a talent for making enemies, and many former allies often found themselves subjected to sharp denunciations for daring to disagree with him. Compared with his Young Ireland contemporaries, he seems to have little of the idealism and generosity of Thomas Davis, the statesmanlike dignity of William Smith O'Brien, or the political pragmatism of Charles Gavan Duffy.

But Mitchel was more than just a hate-filled reactionary. He was one of the most powerful polemical journalists of the nineteenth century, and played a key role in reviving militant Irish nationalism. His views, particularly his fervent denunciations of the hypocrisy of British imperialism and his accusation that the Famine was deliberate genocide, had a lasting influence on nationalist thinking. This biography attempts to discover the origins of Mitchel's views, to examine their influence on Irish nationalism, and to place his anglophobia in a more general critique of the age in which he lived.

CHAPTER I

Youth and Early Life, 1815–45

John Mitchel was born on 3 November 1815 at Camnish, near Dungiven, County Derry, the eldest surviving child of John Mitchel, Presbyterian minister of the Dungiven congregation. John Mitchel senior, descended from Scottish Covenanters, was a prominent figure in Dissenting circles and in 1822 was elected moderator of the Presbyterian Synod of Ulster. A man of liberal political views, he voted for the Whigs but took no active part in politics, devoting himself instead to his religious duties and to charitable works. Deeply involved in the theological controversies that raged in Ulster Presbyterianism, he wrote a number of polemical pamphlets championing Unitarianism. In 1830 he seceded from the Synod of Ulster and became a founder of the Remonstrant Synod of Ulster. In later life John Mitchel junior often claimed that his father had been a United Irishman who had fought during the 1798 rising, but this was an exaggeration. As a boy of fourteen his father had accompanied a party of United Irishmen with a cart of ammunition and was made take the United oath before being allowed to leave. His mother's United Irish connections were rather stronger. Mary Haslett, an intelligent and forceful woman, came from a prominent Derry family and was the daughter of a United Irishman; she was described by Thomas Carlyle as a 'Presbyterian parson's widow of the best Scotch type'.[1]

There were five other children: a son, William, and four daughters, Mary Jane, Matilda, Henrietta and Margaret. In 1819 the family moved to Derry city, where John attended the school conducted by a clergyman, Mr Moore, and proved himself an intelligent and studious pupil. In 1823 they moved to Dromalane, near Newry, County Down, which became their permanent home and the place associated with Mitchel's happiest memories. Here he was educated at the school of a Mr McNiel (where he did not get on well) and at Dr David Henderson's classical school in Newry, where he thrived. At Henderson's he met John Martin, son of a neighbouring large farmer, who became his closest friend and political associate. Mostly, though, he was a solitary child who loved to ramble in the hills around Newry and knew every mountain, stream and glen within walking distance of his home.[2]

He also took a great interest in the theological controversies in which his father engaged. At the age of fourteen he was eagerly scrutinising scriptural and theological texts to refute the arguments of his father's opponents. After leaving Henderson's school in Newry at the age of sixteen, he entered Trinity College, Dublin, on 4 July 1831. He spent little time in Trinity, only travelling there to take the required exams, and made few if any friends at college. Given his son's interest in theological matters, his father believed that he was intent on becoming a clergyman, but during his years at college his religious opinions grew increasingly sceptical, and he eventually declared that he had no vocation for the ministry. Many years later he noted that he had so immersed himself in theological speculation that he had grown sick of it and resolved never again to plunge into 'the abyss of metaphysics'. In the summer of 1834 he went to Derry to work as a clerk in a bank of which his uncle William Haslett was a director. The long hours and dreary work did not suit Mitchel, and he complained to his father that he had no time for study or for his normal leisure pursuits of walking and reading, and his health was suffering. 'Such uninterrupted slavery is intolerable', he protested, and pleaded with his father to be allowed to return home. His state of mind was not helped by the fact that he had fallen in love with a woman from Belfast, six years older than himself. They became secretly engaged, but both families opposed the match, and the couple were forced to part. Mitchel was deeply hurt by the experience and was morose and irritable for many months afterwards; years later when he met the woman unexpectedly he was visibly and powerfully agitated.[3]

He graduated BA from Trinity on 16 February 1836 after an undistinguished academic career. The following Easter he became apprenticed as an attorney to John Henry Quinn of Newry, and during his apprenticeship he met Jane (Jenny) Verner, who was not yet sixteen years old, and fell in love with her. Jenny had been raised by Captain James Verner of Newry, although there were rumours that he was not actually her father. Captain Verner was a landowner and former army officer, and brother of Sir William Verner, a leading County Down Orangeman. In November 1836 the young couple eloped and took the boat to Liverpool. Following in hot pursuit, Captain Verner found them at Chester and promptly had Mitchel arrested. Mitchel spent eighteen days in Kilmainham jail in Dublin, although the charge of abduction against him was eventually dropped. The young lovers were not discouraged and eloped again; on 2 February 1837 they were secretly married in the parish church of Drumcree, County Armagh. Jenny was disowned by the Verners; but although Mitchel's parents also strongly disapproved of his conduct, they accepted his young wife into their family, and the couple settled in Newry, close to the family home.[4] Mitchel afterwards felt considerable remorse for the way in which he had tried the forbearance of his parents. On his father's death in February 1840 he noted in a tone of great sadness: 'I put more grey hairs on that head than ever time did'.[5]

On 3 June 1839, after completing his legal training, Mitchel was sworn in as an attorney and formed a partnership with Samuel Fraser, a successful Newry attorney, and was entrusted with founding a branch office at nearby Banbridge, where he moved. Though he had no great liking for his profession, he applied himself diligently and began to build up a successful practice. He occasionally contributed essays to a Newry literary society and took some interest in politics. He and John Martin, who farmed 400 acres at Loughorne a few miles away, passed much of their time in literary and philosophic discussion; they admired the works of William Cobbett and Walter Scott, but Thomas Carlyle's *The French Revolution* (1837) was their particular favourite. Mitchel thought it 'the profoundest book, and the most eloquent and fascinating history, that English literature ever produced'.[6] Mitchel and Martin became and remained close friends, despite their strongly different temperaments. Mitchel was intense, stern and uncompromising; Martin was calm, quiet and conciliatory – 'a man who would say a good word of the devil himself', noted a contemporary. Perhaps because of these differences, they grew to rely on each other: Martin was one of the few people whose advice Mitchel valued, and when he worked for the *Nation* he often wrote to him seeking his assistance. The fact that they both suffered from asthma also drew them closer together. Mitchel's asthma began about 1839, while Martin was a long-time sufferer, and during his bouts of illness Mitchel often looked after him.[7]

Banbridge was occasionally the scene of sectarian violence after Orange marches, and in the legal proceedings that followed Mitchel was frequently employed by Catholics. The cases were often decided by magistrates who were themselves Orangemen, and Mitchel grew increasingly indignant at the injustices suffered by Catholics. Known locally for their nationalist sympathies, Mitchel and Martin in 1839 helped to organise a public dinner for

Daniel O'Connell in Newry, and they subscribed to the *Nation* newspaper on its launch in October 1842. In 1841 Mitchel first met Charles Gavan Duffy, a Monaghan Catholic and editor of the *Belfast Vindicator*, a pro-Catholic Belfast paper. Duffy was impressed 'by the vigour and liberality of his opinions, as well as by his culture and suavity'. He described Mitchel as

> rather above the middle size, well-made and with a face which was thoughtful and comely, though pensive blue eyes and masses of soft brown hair, a stray ringlet of which he had the habit of twining round his finger while he spoke, gave it, perhaps, too feminine a cast. He lived much alone, and this training had left the ordinary results; he was silent and retiring, slow to speak and apt to deliver his opinion in a form which would be abrupt and dogmatic if it were not relieved by a pleasant smile.[8]

Mitchel occasionally visited Dublin on business, and during one of these visits, probably in the autumn of 1842, Duffy introduced him to Thomas Davis and John Blake Dillon, his co-founders of the *Nation*. Mitchel became close to both men, Davis in particular exerting a strong fascination on him. Mitchel was increasingly drawn into the *Nation* group and contributed his first article in February 1843. That May he joined the Repeal Association and soon was caught up in the excitement of O'Connell's great monster meetings, sharing the bitter disappointment of many nationalists when a government proclamation forced O'Connell to cancel the Clontarf meeting in October. He also shared in the general nationalist indignation when O'Connell was charged with conspiracy and sentenced to twelve months' imprisonment in May 1844, and that summer he was chosen by a County Down public meeting to present an address of sympathy to the imprisoned O'Connell in Richmond jail.[9]

Over the next couple of years his connections with the *Nation* group strengthened. When Davis founded the '82 Club in April 1845, he invited Mitchel to sit on its council. The club, resplendent in its military-style green and gold uniform, was clearly intended as a potential officer corps for the nationalist movement. He was also invited by Duffy to write a biography of Hugh O'Neill for the *Nation*'s 'Library of Ireland' series. These bonds were further strengthened when in autumn Mitchel, Martin, Duffy and John O'Hagan, a Newry barrister, went on a walking tour of Ulster and grew closer as they discussed their visions of Irish cultural and political independence.[10]

Increasingly, differences were emerging in the Repeal Association between O'Connell and the *Nation* group, often known as 'Young Ireland'. The idealistic Young Irelanders sought to forge an inclusive and high-principled Irish nationalism and were often uneasy with what they saw as O'Connell's demagoguery, his close identification with Catholicism, and his political wheeling and dealing. After his release from prison in September 1844 they were suspicious that a chastened O'Connell was intent on renewing his alliance with the Whigs and rowing back on repeal. The Young Irelanders believed that only self-government could bring about national renewal and regarded repeal as non-negotiable; they were certainly not prepared to countenance a Whig reform package as a substitute. The *Nation* criticised O'Connell's attempts to find a federal solution to bridge the gap between the extremes of repeal and unionism, and in May 1845 sharp differences emerged between O'Connell and Davis on the Irish Colleges Bill. The Catholic hierarchy had criticised the proposed new 'Queen's Colleges' on the grounds that they were outside their control and that government failed to provide funds for the teaching of Catholic theology, and O'Connell backed them in denouncing the colleges as 'godless'. But the non-denominational nature of the proposed colleges appealed to most Young Irelanders who were keen to see young Irishmen of all faiths associating freely together. The mutual regard of O'Connell and Davis allowed them to paper over the cracks, and months later divisions were set aside as both sides united in grief at the death of Thomas Davis, aged only thirty, in September 1845.

Mitchel was devastated by Davis's death and believed that the Young Irelanders had lost their 'very heart and soul'. Some weeks afterwards he was chosen by the '82 Club to deliver a eulogy on Davis, but his inexperience as a public speaker and the emotion of the occasion proved too much for him and he was unable to deliver his oration. Distraught as Mitchel was at Davis's death, it nevertheless opened an opportunity for him. His *Life of Aodh O'Neill* had just been published and was well received. In October Duffy offered him the salaried position of assistant editor of the *Nation*, to which he would also be a chief contributor. Although Mitchel had worked hard to establish his solicitor's practice, his heart was never really in an occupation in which he spent his time 'arguing eternally with "shrill attorney logic" about less than nothing, and pocketing fees for the same', and he readily accepted Duffy's offer.[11] He and his family moved to Dublin, taking a house on Upper Leeson Street on 9 October 1845.

CHAPTER 2

The Nation, 1845-7

For the next two years Mitchel wrote most of the *Nation*'s political articles. After the quiet of Banbridge he enjoyed his years in Dublin: for the first time in his life he was in congenial employment, and he formed close friendships with like-minded men. He threw himself vigorously into his work with the *Nation*, and during Duffy's regular absences due to illness, Mitchel assumed full editorial responsibilities. His forceful, pungent journalism introduced an increasingly strident and aggressive note into the paper, most notably in his response to the Tory *Morning Herald*, which advocated severe measures to deal with repeal agitation in Ireland, and noted that newly constructed railways would allow the authorities to deploy large numbers of troops rapidly to any trouble spots. Mitchel's reply intimated that steep railway defiles were ideal ambush points and that the wood and iron used to lay tracks would furnish excellent pike-making materials.[1] The authorities were outraged and immediately undertook a prosecution for sedition against Duffy as the paper's proprietor. The case went to court in June 1846, with Mitchel acting as defence attorney, and Duffy was acquitted. But the article had also offended O'Connell. Mitchel had advocated that instructions on disrupting railways could be read out by repeal wardens throughout Ireland, which irritated O'Connell sufficiently for him to call to the *Nation* office to protest. The *Nation* was forced to disclaim any control over repeal wardens in its next issue. Mitchel, though, had made an enemy of O'Connell, and some weeks later O'Connell pointedly observed at a public meeting that he had admired the *Nation* more 'in the time of the illustrious dead'.[2]

Mitchel, however, continued to make sharp swipes at the British government, particularly after the arrival of the potato blight in Ireland in September 1845 created the prospect of famine in much of the country. He wrote that he expected the current coercion bill going through parliament to pass without any resistance: however much Whigs and Tories differed on 'the propriety of feeding the Irish people, they agree most cordially in the policy of taxing, prosecuting and hanging them'. With conditions deteriorating in many rural districts as famine began to take hold, Mitchel wrote that the Irish people blamed 'the greedy and cruel policy of England': 'Their starving children cannot sit down to their scanty meal but they see the harpy claw of England in their dish. They behold their own wretched food melting in rottenness off the face of the earth: and they see heavy-laden ships, freighted with the yellow corn their own hands have sown and reaped, spreading all sail *for England*; they see it, and with every grain of that corn goes a heavy curse.' An article on insurrection in Poland declared: 'Better a little blood-letting to show that there is blood, than a patient dragging of chains.'[3] Some Young Irelanders, notably John O'Hagan and John Edward Pigot, complained to Duffy of the *Nation*'s increasingly violent tone, and he was moved to remonstrate with Mitchel: 'You write of insurrections as if they were made to order in the back office of a newspaper.'[4]

Mitchel was becoming an increasingly prominent political figure, chairing a meeting of the Repeal Association for the first time in March 1846. He was also one of a deputation of six selected in April 1846 by the '82 Club to visit the Irish MP William Smith O'Brien, who had been imprisoned for contempt after refusing to sit on a parliamentary railway committee on the grounds that his only concern was with Irish legislation. O'Brien, a substantial landlord and former Tory, often acted as a mediating voice between Young Ireland and 'Old Ireland' as represented by O'Connell, and half-jokingly dubbed himself 'Middle-aged Ireland'. The deputation visited the incarcerated O'Brien in the cellar of Westminster and presented him with an address of support. Mitchel noted proudly that the cellar was the only part of the Houses of Parliament that he ever visited on this, his first and last visit to London.[5] While there he took the opportunity to visit his hero Thomas Carlyle at Chelsea and was received cordially. Several Young Irelanders, Mitchel in particular, regarded Carlyle as a prophetic voice crying out amidst the hypocrisy and banality of the age. Some months earlier Mitchel had praised Carlyle in the *Nation* as 'our venerated and beloved preceptor at whose feet we have long studied and learned' and maintained that it was mainly Carlyle who had inspired him to become 'a determined Repealer and Irish nationalist'. Yet that evening he was overawed by Carlyle's presence and appalled by his dismissal of Irish grievances and his uncompromising 'might is right' philosophy.[6]

But Carlyle remained a profound influence on Mitchel, who borrowed much of his unshakeable moral conviction and his suspicion of Enlightenment rationalism and *laissez-faire* political economy. He also borrowed Carlyle's declamatory style and his habit of dismissing those opposed to him as canting hypocrites, a tendency that could easily descend into rant. The main criticism that Duffy and Davis had about the first draft of his *Life of Aodh O'Neill* was its excess of Carlylean phrases, most of which they persuaded him to remove.[7] Even Mitchel's decision to write on O'Neill probably owed something to Carlyle's emphasis on the importance of heroic figures in nation building. Carlyle returned Mitchel's visit in September 1846 and later recalled that 'His frugally elegant small house and table pleased me much, as did the man himself, a fine, elastic-spirited young fellow . . . on whom all my persuasions were thrown away.' He often read Mitchel's articles in the *Nation*, and although there was much in them he liked, he thought them 'wild' and they caused him 'ever greater pain'. He regarded Mitchel as 'a noble, chivalrous fellow, full of talent and manful temper of every kind. In fact I love him very much, and must infinitely regret to see the like of him enveloped in such poor delusions, partisanships and narrow violences, very unworthy of him.' Carlyle told him 'he would most likely be hanged, but I told him they could not hang the immortal part of him'.[8]

In July 1846 the differences between O'Connell and Young Ireland finally came to a head. After the failed prosecution of Duffy for Mitchel's railway article in June, O'Connell took the opportunity to propose that the Repeal Association sever all connections with newspapers and reassert its commitment exclusively to peaceful political agitation. Impatient at sniping from the 'juvenile orators' of Young Ireland, O'Connell was anxious to pour cold water on the increasingly bellicose rhetoric of the *Nation* and to demonstrate that he was still in full control of the association. The latter intention was given additional urgency by the collapse of Sir Robert Peel's ministry and the accession to power of the Whigs on 30 June 1846. In the preceding months O'Connell had stepped up co-operation with the Whigs, and it seemed possible that he might conclude a pact to trade repeal for a more benign administration in Dublin Castle and some influential places for his followers.

At a Repeal Association meeting on 13 July O'Connell moved a resolution that all its members repudiate the use of physical force to attain political objectives. As nobody was actually advocating violence there and then, the debate focused on the abstract point of whether physical force had been justifiable in the past or would be

in the future. Several Young Irelanders, notably Thomas Francis
Meagher, gave full rein to their oratorical powers and refused to
'stigmatise the sword' that had freed nations such as the Americans
and Belgians from foreign domination. Meagher argued that there
were times 'when political amelioration calls for a drop of blood –
and many thousand drops of blood . . . Be it for the defence, or be it
for the assertion of a nation's liberty, I look upon the sword as a
sacred weapon.' Mitchel, who had by now become an effective
public speaker, took a leading part in the debate. He stated his
wholehearted approval of the Repeal Association pursuing its aims
by peaceful methods, but he was not prepared to accept a blanket
condemnation of physical force at all times and in all circumstances.
This, for example, would involve condemning the Volunteers of
1782, who had taken up arms to assert their rights; the founding
fathers of America, who achieved their liberty through armed rebellion; and even the United Irishmen. 'My father', Mitchel noted,
'was a United Irishman. The men of '98 thought liberty worth
some blood-letting, and although they failed, it were rather hard
that one of their sons would now be thought unworthy to unite in
a peaceful struggle for the independence of his country, unless he
will proclaim that he "abhors" the memory of his own father.'[9] His
speech lacked Meagher's oratorical histrionics but was all the more
effective for it; Duffy described it as 'savage in its plainness',
recalling that 'his clear strong sentences fell like strokes of the
short Roman sword, lopping and maiming wherever they lighted'.[10]

Most Young Irelanders believed that the peace resolutions were
an attempt to expel them from the association and were reluctant
to take the bait. But during the debates much of the bad blood that
had festered between the idealistic Young Irelanders and the
populist O'Connellites emerged, and the tone grew increasingly
bitter. O'Connell accused Mitchel of 'instigating the country to
anarchy and violence'. Mitchel retorted by claiming openly that

the resolutions were a pretext to expel opponents of a Whig alliance, and he warned against imposing unnecessary tests that could only weaken the association: 'I am one of the Saxon Irishmen of the North. And you want that race of Irishmen in your ranks more than any others.' After several days of debate Tom Steele, the O'Connellite chairman, called on Mitchel and Meagher to repudiate physical force without any qualification or ambiguity. They refused, and with Smith O'Brien, Duffy and many others walked out of the meeting and out of the Repeal Association, after which O'Connell's resolution was overwhelmingly carried.[11]

For his part, Mitchel was glad the breach had finally been made. He maintained that O'Connell had told followers before the debates that he wanted to expel Mitchel and anyone holding similar opinions. He claimed that the public knew the resolutions were 'humbug' and that there was considerable sympathy for the Young Irelanders. Mitchel opposed any attempts at reconciliation, and when such efforts were made several months later, he published a statement in the *Nation* rebuffing them. He believed that these moves to heal the split were not made in good faith, and he dismissed the O'Connellites as crypto-Whigs and place-hunters.[12]

By this time, however, most of the Irish people had more pressing concerns. The potato blight had reappeared in July 1846, and over the next couple of months the crop failed disastrously, creating the prospect of mass starvation for the millions dependent on potatoes. The relief measures of the Whig government were wholly inadequate and were regularly attacked by Mitchel in the *Nation*. Ireland's salvation, he claimed, lay not in the provision of paltry alms but in giving Ireland 'control of her own resources, the making of her own laws, the enjoyment of the fruits of her own industry'.[13]

In December 1846 an attempt was made to hold a conference to heal the divisions between nationalists in the face of this catastrophe, but neither side showed any real willingness to compromise

and it failed. Instead in January 1847 the Young Irelanders decided to found their own organisation, the Irish Confederation,
intended to encompass Irishmen of all creeds and classes. It placed
special emphasis on recruiting the landed gentry into the nationalist cause. Mitchel became a member of the Confederation's
council which determined its policy. To harness public opinion,
Confederate clubs were to be founded throughout the country.
Mostly, though, these took root only in Dublin and other towns
and cities, usually attracting politically conscious artisans, clerks
and students.[14]

By now the meagre reserves of the Irish peasantry were exhausted
after two successive crop failures, and deaths from famine and fever
mounted inexorably. The extent of the disaster bewildered most
observers, but in the spring of 1847 the *Nation* published a series
of articles advocating radical solutions to Ireland's agrarian problems. They were written by the hitherto unknown James Fintan
Lalor, the crippled son of a substantial Queen's County farmer and
former O'Connellite MP. Lalor argued that the catastrophe of the
Famine had dissolved Irish rural society 'and another requires to
be constituted'. All efforts should be directed at creating a secure
and independent peasantry, the foundation of all prosperity.
Landlords were offered the opportunity to participate in creating
this new society, but were warned that 'you are far less important to
the people than the people are to you' and that they would be swept
aside if they did not co-operate.[15]

Since January 1847 Lalor had also engaged in private corres-
pondence with several leading Confederates, notably Duffy and
Mitchel, in which he was much more specific about his aims and
means. He argued that repeal had little relevance to the famine-
stricken Irish peasantry, and that the Confederation should concentrate on the issue of greatest importance to the Irish masses, the
land question. In doing so they would adopt a practical programme

linking agrarian grievances directly to the campaign for political independence. Previously most agrarian reformers had simply sought 'tenant right' – a greater degree of security of tenure – but Lalor wanted more. He argued that the title to land derived not from the crown but from the nation, and that therefore tenant farmers co-owned the land with its nominal proprietors. Knowing full well that landlords would never willingly grant tenants co-ownership, Lalor advocated a nationwide rent strike and physical resistance to evictions until they did. In seeking 'the soil of Ireland for the people of Ireland', Lalor wanted to repeal the 'entire conquest of seven hundred years – a thing much more easily done than to repeal the Union'.[16]

Mitchel was strongly attracted to Lalor's views and, having pondered them for some weeks, adopted them with the zeal of a convert. However, he still regarded the landed gentry as the natural leaders of the Irish people and hoped that Lalor's proposals could be implemented with their co-operation to minimise social upheaval. Writing to Smith O'Brien, he argued that if Irish landlords were willing to concede tenant right and accept some form of co-ownership, they could 'become the most popular and powerful aristocracy on earth . . . [and] save this nation and themselves at the same time'.[17] Mitchel's hope that the landed gentry could be persuaded of the benefits of tenant right and self-government led him in June 1847 to take a leading part in the Irish Council, a body founded to draw landlords into the repeal agitation and take more effective action to relieve the famine.

That month Lalor wrote directly to Mitchel, remonstrating with him for not acting forcibly enough on his ideas, and claiming that the landlords were 'aliens and enemies' who had spurned their chance to become part of the nation.[18] Mitchel, though, still clung to the hope that an agreement could be reached with the landlords. If this could be done, it would be possible to 'take the people out of the hands of Lalor and of all the revolutionists. But the time has come when affairs must take a decisive turn either in one way or the other. I sincerely hope it will be in the moderate direction.'[19] Over the next few months, however, he became steadily disillusioned with the Irish Council. It gave no support to a motion to keep the harvest in the country to feed the starving, and fewer and fewer landlords bothered to attend. In November 1847 the Council finally presented its report on landlord–tenant relations. It conceded little to tenant farmers, simply offering them compensation for substantial improvements to their holdings, and avoided tackling the substantive question of tenant right. Mitchel attempted to amend the report to recognise legally the Ulster custom of security of tenure and extend it throughout Ireland, but he was voted down. The final straw for him came later that month when Irish landlords, frightened at growing levels of agrarian crime, called on the government for a strong coercion bill, a measure that Mitchel believed 'was merely an engine to crush tenant right, and all other popular right, and to enable the landlords to eject, distrain and exterminate in peace and security'. He dismissed the deliberations of the Council as a sham and, regarding himself as betrayed, turned sharply against the landed classes.[20]

As the famine worsened during the winter of 1847–8, the sufferings experienced by the Irish peasantry radicalised Mitchel's politics and sharpened his resentment towards the British government. Earlier that year, while travelling to Galway with some Young Ireland colleagues to support the repeal candidate in a by-election, he saw scenes of suffering and desolation that appalled him. He recalled 'little children leaning against a fence when the sun shone out – for they could not stand – their limbs fleshless, their bodies half-naked, their faces bloated yet wrinkled, and of a pale, greenish hue – children who would never, it was too plain, grow up to be men and women. I saw Trevelyan's claw in the vitals of those

children: his red tape would draw them to death: in his government laboratory he had prepared for them the typhus poison.'[21]

Writing in the *Nation*, Mitchel began to formulate his theory of
the Famine.[22] He argued that it was not primarily a natural disaster,
but a deliberate attempt to exterminate the Irish peasantry. Certainly
the potato crop had failed, but how could a country be suffering
from famine when in fact it was well stocked with food and continued to export tons of wheat, oats, beef and butter? People were
starving because the British government had taken advantage of
the potato failure to pursue its diabolical plans. To feed Britain's
ever-expanding industrial population, Ireland was to be converted
into a vast cattle and wheat farm. Its 'surplus population', farming
their myriad smallholdings, was an obstacle in the way of British
progress. But hunger would soon clear them from the land and
send them to the poorhouse, the coffin-ship or the grave. Ireland,
shorn of its fractious peasantry, would be easier to govern and
reconciled to its role within the United Kingdom – the discontented
masses mobilised by O'Connell would be no more. England would
gain in every way.

The Famine was the pivotal event in Mitchel's career. How was
it, he asked, that such a catastrophe could happen under the rule of
the most powerful and prosperous state on earth, which proclaimed itself as the vanguard of nineteenth-century progress? He
concluded that both the British Empire and the progressive ideals
it claimed to represent stood indicted as hypocritical shams, and he
resolved to do his utmost to reveal them as such. He claimed that
'A kind of sacred wrath took possession of a few Irishmen at this
period. They could endure the horrible scene no longer, and
resolved to cross the path of the British car of conquest, though it
should crush them to atoms.'[23]

Mitchel was wrong on a number of counts. Irish grain exports
decreased considerably during the Famine years, while imports of

food soared. He greatly exaggerated the deliberateness of British policy, which tended to respond to events rather than operate to a preordained plan, and he gave little credit to government officials who conscientiously strove to alleviate the effects of the Famine. But, although overstated, some of Mitchel's charges contained a grain of truth. Had food exports been stopped after the disastrous harvest of 1846 and before the import of large quantities of foreign grain in 1847, then the worst effects of the Famine could have been alleviated. The throwing of all the costs of famine relief on to Irish taxpayers from mid-1847, and the insistence that hungry people should carry out heavy labour on relief works of dubious value, showed that the British government was indeed capable of acting selfishly and callously. The government had often shown itself more eager to defend private property and to pass coercion acts than undertake effectual efforts to relieve the Famine, and, since relief was generally only given to those who had surrendered their smallholdings, it could be interpreted as encouraging systematic land clearances. Many British officials did in fact see the failure of the potato as a heaven-sent opportunity for implementing a programme of social engineering that would catapult Ireland's backward agriculture into the modern age of capitalist farming. Sir Charles Edward Trevelyan, the assistant secretary of the Treasury and one of the most doctrinaire advocates of *laissez-faire* political economy, maintained that the famine was 'a direct stroke of an all-wise and all-merciful Providence' and 'the sharp but effectual remedy by which the cure is likely to be effected'.[24] Such views were held at the highest level by men such as Sir Charles Wood, the Chancellor of the Exchequer, and by a host of lesser officials. England may not have created the famine, but some British officials did exploit famine conditions to advance their programme of reform. For the political economists of the Treasury, Ireland's difficulty was England's opportunity.

The accusation that the Famine was deliberate genocide was not unique to Mitchel, but it was he who expressed this idea most forcefully and memorably. In *The Last Conquest of Ireland (Perhaps)* (1861), he maintained that '[A] million and half of men, women, and children were carefully, prudently, and peacefully *slain* by the English government. They died of hunger in the midst of abundance, which their own hands created.' Dismissing those who explained these events as a divine judgement on the Irish people, he observed: 'The Almighty indeed sent the potato blight, but the English created the Famine.'[25] This became his most lasting contribution to Irish nationalism, seeping deep into popular consciousness at home and abroad and creating a visceral hatred of the British government.[26]

Mitchel was deeply concerned with the moral as well as the physical effects of the Famine. As a nationalist who extolled the character and culture of his people, he was most anxious that they should not be seen as craven beggars, and claimed that the poor laws were being used to demoralise and enslave them. After a model soup-kitchen opened at the Royal Barracks in Dublin where the poor lapped up their food with chained spoons as Castle officials and Dublin society looked on, he winced with humiliation and exclaimed: 'Oh Ireland! Ireland! has the very soul withered out of us?' Much of Mitchel's rage at the Famine stemmed from a sense of shame that the Irish peasantry had accepted their fate with passivity. Not only Irish lives, but Irish honour was being sacrificed, and he called on those who were left to take action to save themselves 'that we, too, may not be flung into coffinless graves, amid the bitter scorn and contemptuous laughter of mankind'. Looking back some years later, he admitted that he had acted less out of love for Ireland and more out of 'scornful impatience at the thought that I had the misfortune, I and my children, to be born in a country, which suffered itself to be oppressed and humiliated by another'.[27]

He burned with anger that even in these conditions the Irish people had refused to rise up against those responsible for their sufferings: 'Which is the more hideous evil – three seasons of famine-slaughter in the midst of heaven's abundance, at the point of foreign bayonets, with all its train of debasing diseases and more debasing vices, or a thirty years' war to scourge the stranger from your soil, though it leave that soil a smoking wilderness?' Mitchel blamed the lethargy of the Irish peasantry primarily on O'Connell, who he claimed had used his eloquence to emasculate and demoralise them. It was Mitchel above all who bequeathed to militant nationalism the notion that O'Connell's advocacy of peaceful agitation had misled and bewildered the Irish people: O'Connell was 'next to the British government, the worst enemy that Ireland ever had – or rather the most fatal friend'. To jolt the Catholic peasantry out of their moral-force trance, Mitchel attempted to shame them into action: 'Die – die in your patience and perseverance; but be well assured of this – that the priest who bids you perish patiently amidst your own golden harvests preaches the gospel of England, insults manhood and common sense, bears false witness against religion, and blasphemes the providence of God.'[28]

By the autumn of 1847, Mitchel's views were diverging increasingly from those of his Confederation colleagues. He had by now completely adopted Lalor's proposals for a rent strike, and called for the withholding of poor rates as well. On a number of occasions his editorials made thinly veiled calls for a national insurrection.[29] Increasingly Duffy was forced to censor his articles, much to the disgust of Mitchel who believed that the situation demanded 'more and more unmitigated plain speaking'.[30] Sharp differences were also emerging between Mitchel and Duffy in the Confederation. In November they had both been appointed to a committee to draft proposals for future action. On 1 December Duffy produced a plan that argued for constitutional actions by all classes of Irishmen to achieve repeal, which was endorsed strongly by the Confederation's council. Mitchel strongly dissented, and a week later he resigned from the *Nation*.

Mitchel wrote to Lalor admitting that he had been wrong on the question of winning over landlords to the national cause. He accepted that the Irish Council was a 'mere fraud and delusion' and claimed that Duffy had prevented him for some time from fully expounding his revolutionary views in the *Nation*. 'The *Nation*, I fear has fallen into the merest old-womanly drivelling and snivelling, and the people are without a friend at the press.' He believed the Confederation was on the wrong path, and he resolved 'to change its milk and water course or else to destroy it as a nuisance. It is better to reduce the island to a cinder than let it rot into an obscure quagmire, peopled with reptiles.'[31]

By now Mitchel was completely disillusioned with constitutional agitation. The bribery and intimidation he had witnessed at the Galway by-election in February 1847 had soured parliamentary politics for him. He was opposed to the Confederation contesting the 1847 general election, writing to O'Brien that 'we have neither the men, the money nor the franchises' and that most of the Irish people were so intent on survival that they had little interest in 'electing members to sit in so palpably useless and delusional an assembly'.[32] The poor showing in the election confirmed his view – only two Confederates were elected, and many of the 36 Repealers returned were distinctly lukewarm towards self-government and willing to accept government office.

Appealing to the wider membership of the Confederation for support, he maintained that Ireland was already in 'a state of war – a war of "property" against poverty – a war of "law" against life'. He argued that the peasantry should not trust in laws or parliaments but only in 'their own individual rights, defend those to the last, and sell their lives and lands as dear as they could'.

Constitutional action was simply a dissipation of effort – fighting the battle on ground chosen by the enemy. Instead the Confederation and the *Nation* should begin to disseminate instructions on guerrilla warfare. At the Confederation's anniversary meeting on 12 January 1848 Mitchel further underlined his radicalism by expressing solidarity with the Chartists (whose democratic ideals were regarded warily by most Irish nationalists), maintaining that they and the Confederates had a common enemy in the British oligarchy.[33]

The moderate Smith O'Brien was horrified by Mitchel's rhetoric. He complained that Mitchel and a few fellow 'mutineers' were trying to subvert the Confederation and turn it into a revolutionary body.[34] He was particularly concerned that the militant sentiments being expressed by Mitchel and his young disciple Thomas Devin Reilly, a former journalist on the *Nation*, would be attributed to the Confederation as a whole. He therefore proposed a series of resolutions, condemning armed insurrection and the refusal to pay rent and rates, and reiterating that the Confederation was committed to obtaining legislative independence 'by the force of opinion' and 'the combination of all classes of Irishmen'.[35]

From 2 to 4 February 1848 the Confederation debated its future policy in the Rotunda in Dublin. Most speakers supported O'Brien's resolutions, but Mitchel argued that the selfish conduct of landlords had effectively excluded them from the national movement and that constitutional methods had already proved themselves useless. He had trusted the Irish gentry and had been betrayed: 'I would have followed the aristocracy of Ireland in the march to freedom with zeal and loyalty, if they had only led. But they cheated me – they cheated you – and they are now laughing at us all.' Mitchel claimed O'Brien's resolutions were new 'peace resolutions' designed to exclude militants from the Confederation in the same way that the Young Irelanders had been forced out of the Repeal

Association. He maintained that the Confederation should encompass a variety of opinions, and that he simply interpreted 'force of opinion' in a broader manner than O'Brien: 'Must the force of opinion always be legal? – always be peaceful? Does opinion then mean law? . . . I hold that there is no opinion in Ireland worth a farthing which is not illegal. I hold that armed opinion is a thousand times stronger than unarmed.'[36]

Eighteen months on from the debates in the Repeal Association, differences in the Confederation were again crystallising around the question of physical force. But for Mitchel the catastrophe of the Famine had given more than abstract relevance to the issue. He believed that if the Irish peasantry were to be exterminated, it was better for them to die fighting than face painful and ignominious death through starvation and disease. Mitchel made clear that he was not proposing immediate insurrection but a campaign of militant passive resistance, involving refusal to pay rent and poor rates and forcible resistance to evictions, that would bring the Irish countryside to boiling-point until eventually it would erupt in spontaneous insurrection.

Speaker after speaker rose to challenge Mitchel's arguments, including Confederates who had been close to him in the past, such as Meagher, Richard O'Gorman and Michael Doheny. Adopting Mitchel's policy, they maintained, would mean throwing away the support of landlords and the middle class merely to gain the fragment of the peasantry prepared to defy their priests. Moreover, most of the peasantry were in no position to mount an insurrection but were (according to Doheny) 'sicklied, hungry, wasted, exiled, or in their graves'. Any insurrection would be local-ised and easily defeated, and blood would be shed in vain. The Confederation's support was mainly confined to the towns, and even there they were well outnumbered by O'Connellites. Mitchel's opponents maintained that he knew nothing of the peasantry, and they knew nothing of him. 'The people of Munster', exclaimed Meagher, 'know as little of Mitchel as of Mahomet!'[37]

Duffy, stung by some sharp criticisms from Mitchel, was particularly scathing. He claimed that the 'liberty of opinion' sought by Mitchel and Reilly was 'liberty to ruin the national cause' and would result in 'chaos and destruction'. O'Gorman dismissed Mitchel and Reilly as 'Infant Ireland'. On 4 February O'Brien's resolutions were adopted by 317 votes to 188.[38] Mitchel, Reilly and Martin withdrew from the Confederation's council, but they remained members of the Confederation and continued to build up their support among the clubs. As Mitchel could no longer use the Confederation to propagate his views, he decided to set up a new weekly newspaper of his own, the *United Irishman*.

CHAPTER 3

United Irishman, 1848

If, as a wag remarked, the tone of the *Nation* was Wolfe Tone, then the tone of the *United Irishman* was Wolfe Tone at his most democratic and desperate. For its masthead Mitchel adopted Tone's famous dictum: 'If the men of property will not support us, they must fall; we can support ourselves by the aid of that numerous and respectable class of the community – the men of no property.' Mitchel was editor and leader writer, and his friends Martin, Reilly, Father John Kenyon and James Clarence Mangan also contributed, Mitchel describing them as 'Catholics, Protestants, and Pagans, but all resolute revolutionists'.[1] Mangan, whom Mitchel had come to know when he was editing the *Nation*, occasionally contributed verse to the *United Irishman*. Mitchel was one of the few people with whom the morbidly shy poet would converse, and his politics strongly influenced Mangan, encouraging him to give vent to his pent-up resentment against British imperialism. After Mangan's death Mitchel became a strong advocate for his work, describing him as 'a rebel with his whole heart and soul against the whole British spirit of the age'.[2]

The first issue of the *United Irishman* was published on 12 February 1848 and caused a sensation, its run of 5,000 copies quickly selling out. It was published at 12 Trinity Street, close to Dublin Castle, and immediately threw down a challenge to the government. Mitchel spurned secret conspiracy and openly proclaimed his intention to overthrow British rule, addressing the Lord Lieutenant, Clarendon, as a 'butcher' and 'high commissioner of spies'. He thundered that the 'holy hatred of foreign dominion which nerved our noble predecessors fifty years ago for the dungeon, the field, or the gallows . . . still lives, thank God! and glows as hot and fierce as ever. To educate that holy hatred . . . I hereby devote the columns of the *United Irishman*.'[3] Such journalism had not been seen in Ireland for fifty years and, according to one observer, 'every word struck with the force and terror of lightning'.[4] There was no talk of combination of classes. Instead Mitchel told the Irish peasantry that the intention of their gentry 'is to murder you, and to rob you, and to divide the spoil between the Irish landlords and the English government'.[5]

Mitchel called openly for national insurrection, maintaining that 'It is a more hideous national calamity for ten men to be cast out to die of hunger, like dogs in ditches, than for ten thousand to be hewn to pieces, fighting like men and Christians in defence of their rights.'[6] The paper regularly contained articles on barricade construction, pike drills and street fighting. One article (written by Thomas Devin Reilly, but approved of by Mitchel), advocated the flinging of vitriol on troops from the windows of houses.[7] This was picked up by Mitchel's enemies and for many years after was thrown back at him as an example of his inhumanity and fanaticism. Mitchel, however, never flung vitriol at anyone; verbal vitriol was much more his style.

Mitchel particularly hoped to draw working-class Ulster Protestants into the nationalist movement. He believed that he had a special understanding of his northern co-religionists, and regularly reminded them that they at least had not been corrupted by O'Connell's moral-force teachings: they had 'never denied the noble creed and sacraments of manhood. *You* have not been schooled for forty years in the false cant of moral force . . . You have not yet learned the litany of slaves, and the whine of beaten hounds, and the way to die a coward's death.' He attempted to persuade them that their common interest was with the farmers and labourers of the south and not with a government and aristocracy that was exploiting the economic crisis to undermine the Ulster custom of tenant right and turn independent farmers into landless labourers, and used religious distinctions to blind them to their true interests: 'The Pope as we know is the "Man of Sin" and the "Antichrist" . . . but he brings no ejectments in Ulster.'[8]

The *United Irishman* ran for just under four months, but it stands as one of the most remarkable newspapers in the history of Irish journalism. Mitchel had full editorial control, and he used it to hammer home his revolutionary message week after week in powerful, hard-hitting prose. No libel lawyers perused the copy of the *United Irishman*; its very aim was to provoke a severe response that would prove the British government paid only lip service to liberal ideals.

The violent propaganda expounded by Mitchel in the *United Irishman* shocked many of his Young Ireland colleagues, who more than ever regarded him as a dangerous incendiary. But towards the end of February 1848 the political situation was transformed by news that a revolution in Paris had overthrown the French monarchy. For moderate Confederates there was much to admire in a near-bloodless revolution that appeared to have been accomplished by the concerted action of all classes. Mitchel's belligerent rhetoric was now seen in a different light. When his Confederation colleagues had rejected his calls for revolution, most had done so not on principle, but on the grounds that the time was not right. Now, with the flame of rebellion spreading and monarchies apparently toppling across Europe, the time seemed to have come.

When a republic was declared in France, Mitchel threw all reserve aside and proclaimed his republicanism: '*Vive la République!*

Yes! the only true form of government – the form which national liberty takes when it belongs to the people, and is not prostituted by a class, the Republic so worshipped by the United Irishmen of old . . . is won at last . . . And so we may have a Republic nearer home ere long: for in these events lies our fate.' Like Lalor, Mitchel now rejected repeal of the union and the semi-independence of the 'constitution of 1782'. 'It vanished in 18 years and I hope we may never see it again . . . Whatever be the opinion of my brother Confederates, there shall be no rest for me until I see Ireland a free republic.'[9] Mitchel made a triumphant return to the Confederation and was loudly cheered, especially by the younger members of the Dublin clubs. He now seemed the man of the moment, and his resolution directing the Confederate clubs to arm themselves was strongly approved. But Duffy, by now a bitter enemy, was not impressed and noted that 'Never was a man so metamorphosed; he used to be a modest and courteous gentleman, now he demeaned himself as if the French revolution and the new opportunities it furnished were his personal achievements.'[10]

All over Ireland great nationalist demonstrations celebrated the new French republic. In early March Mitchel was elected to a committee to organise a public demonstration of solidarity with France. The committee sent an Irish delegation to Paris that included Smith O'Brien and Meagher, and on 3 April presented a fraternal address to Alphonse de Lamartine, minister for foreign affairs in the provisional government. Lamartine was anxious that the fledgling republic should maintain friendly relations with Britain and made a non-committal reply that gave no encouragement to Irish nationalism. Most Irish nationalists were deeply disappointed by the French response, but Mitchel, always anxious that Irishmen should prove themselves worthy of freedom by fighting for it themselves, declared his pleasure 'that M. Lamartine has let us know distinctly we must rely on ourselves'.[11]

Mitchel nevertheless lauded political and social developments in France, claiming that her new government had renounced competition and free trade and enacted legislation to protect labour and legalise workmen's combinations. He maintained that when Ireland became a free and democratic republic, she would protect her working classes by enacting similar legislation. Mitchel equated British rule with heartless *laissez-faire* capitalism and contended that 'The English, or Famine system, must be abolished utterly – in farms and workshops, in town and country, abolished utterly; and to do this were worth three revolutions, or three times three.'[12]

In many of Mitchel's writings there are strong echoes of William Cobbett: in his denunciation of the pervasive corruption of the British ruling oligarchy; in his condemnation of ideologies of 'progress' such as capitalism and utilitarianism; and, most of all, in his defence of the robust self-reliance of the small farmer or independent artisan. Like Cobbett, Mitchel saw modern industrial society as a dehumanising force that destroyed traditional societies. To protect workers from the ravages of capitalism, he advocated a system of economic regulation and mutual obligation between employer and employee. He praised the guilds of the pre-industrial age which he claimed had created a secure working environment for their members, fixing wage rates and working hours, and had established mutual rights and duties between master and man.[13] His idealised social system consisted of sturdily independent artisans in the towns and independent yeomen farmers in the countryside, both enjoying the fruits of their own labour:

I have always looked with a sort of veneration upon an independent farmer cultivating his small demesne – a rural *pater-familias*, who aspires to no lot but labour in his own land, and takes off his hat to no 'superior' under God Almighty. Tenant right, fee-farm, call his tenure what you will, only let him be sure that where he sows, he and his shall eat, reap and be satisfied . . . never troubling his mind about the Progress of the Species, nor knowing in the least what that phrase may mean.[14]

Mitchel argued that since capital was created by the working man, he should be its main beneficiary. But in modern capitalist society the principles of natural justice were reversed: those who toiled to create wealth were labelled 'men of no property', while 'the men who do nothing, who idle the year round – the fools with long bug-a-boo nicknames and gee-gaws, are held to *own* everything'. The *United Irishman* proclaimed that the cause of Irish independence was 'essentially not only a national movement, but also – why not admit it? – a *class movement*'.[15]

Such views, however, stemmed more from Mitchel's hatred of capitalism and landlordism than from any coherent socialist ideology. He explicitly denied preaching 'Socialism, Communism, Fourierism, St Simonism, or any system whatever approaching them' and dismissed Louis Blanc's plans for state-sponsored workshops as 'centralisation in its worst form [which] would interfere in every man's business with a minute despotism more intolerable than that of the old Paris police or the Holy Inquisition'.[16] Mitchel scoffed at utopian socialists such as Owen, Fourier and St Simon, as starry-eyed believers in human progress: 'Heaven knows the social problem in modern Europe has come to be a hard one; but Fourier–Owenism is not the solution.' He was equally dismissive of Marxism many years later. Commenting on the June days in Paris in 1848, he applauded the fact that the left-wing insurrectionists 'were swept from the streets with grape and canister – the only way of dealing with such unhappy creatures . . . Socialists are something worse than wild beasts.'[17]

Just as his social philosophy stressed the independence of the individual, so it stressed decentralisation of power within states and internationally:

For centralisation in a state, as a means of 'human progress' . . . we substitute localisation . . . For communism of men we substitute entire independence of individual man; and instead of a government that does everything, we desire a government that does as little as possible . . . To 'fusion' of peoples we oppose the independence of nations; to communism of nations we oppose isolation – the throwing of each nation on its own resources . . . compelling it to limit its wants and appetites to the resources of its own soil, and the industry of its own people – thus preventing conquest, making telegraphs, railroads, steamboats, mere accidents to its convenience, instead of necessities to its existence.[18]

Despite his enthusiastic advocacy of republicanism, Mitchel later claimed that he cared little about forms of government and was no doctrinaire republican. He had advocated a democratic levelling republicanism in 1848 because he believed that the Irish masses 'cannot be roused in any quarrel less than social revolution, destruction of landlordism, and denial of all tenure and title derived from English sovereigns'.[19] In adopting republicanism he was also laying claim to the legacy of the United Irishmen, who had made the most formidable effort to establish Irish independence in recent history. Like the United Irishmen, the Young Irelanders were influenced by the tradition of classical republicanism and sought to transform the Irish masses into a virtuous self-reliant citizenry, rather than a gullible mob blindly following a charismatic leader. To accomplish this, Thomas Davis stressed the role of education, but Mitchel put the emphasis on armed conflict: the Irish people must prove themselves worthy of freedom. Their apparent passivity in the face of famine and starvation clearly demonstrated that they lacked the martial virtue of the self-reliant citizen. Mitchel exhorted the Irish masses to procure arms (the badge of citizenship in the classical republican tradition) and learn their use. Before any general insurrection, he maintained, 'there must first be sound manly doctrine preached and embraced. And next, there must be many desultory collisions with British troops, both in town and country, and the sight of clear steel, and of blood smoking hot, must become familiar.'[20] The fruit of this struggle would be possession of their own land, which in turn would consolidate their status as independent and self-reliant citizens. The concept of citizenship was of the utmost importance for Mitchel (it would feature prominently in the titles of his newspapers), and, in keeping with the classical republican tradition, he emphasised duties rather than rights. The first lecture he delivered after his arrival in the United States in 1853 was 'The Duties of Adopted Citizens' in which he argued that the citizen 'belongs absolutely and exclusively to the state . . . [which] has a clear title to his sole and undivided allegiance'.[21]

Although Mitchel sought to link his republicanism with that of the United Irishmen, there were significant differences between them. The United Irishmen had little of Mitchel's anglophobia and their writings did not revel in violence as his did. Their nationalism owed much to the Enlightenment ideal of humanity progressing towards a universal future of liberty and fraternity. Mitchel's nationalism drew on more romantic roots: it stressed the power of emotion rather than reason, the destructive potential of human nature rather than its capacity for progress, and the historical differences between nations rather than their common aspirations.

Around this time Lamartine's *History of the Girondists* was widely read, and many readers equated particular actors in Irish politics with famous French Revolutionary figures: Mitchel was invariably identified as Robespierre, 'the country lawyer, accepted as their chief by the Jacobins of Paris, because he was always more Jacobin than they'.[22] But as Mitchel's calls for revolution became ever stronger, many Confederates were deeply uncomfortable with this Robespierre in their midst, and especially with his violent attacks on landlordism and private property. The government too was nervous, and three days after the Dublin demonstration on 20 March 1848 in favour of the revolution in France, Mitchel, O'Brien and Meagher were charged with making seditious speeches, though all three were given bail. O'Brien believed that the government had deliberately chosen to prosecute him with Mitchel in order to discredit him by association with Mitchel's views. Although the two men were on good personal terms, O'Brien strongly resented any identification with Mitchel, a man he claimed was regarded as a 'bloodthirsty villain' by many.[23] He believed that Mitchel's writings in the *United Irishman* had done much to alienate the middle and upper classes from the Confederation: they 'interpreted the doctrines of the *United Irishman* as stimulants to plunder' and 'now began to regard the agitation for repeal as synonymous with a confiscation of property'. He notified Mitchel that he would never again appear on the same platform as him. Mitchel accepted his position, but through a misunderstanding both men were present at a nationalist meeting in Limerick on 29 April. The meeting was disrupted by an O'Connellite crowd infuriated by a recent attack in the *United Irishman* on O'Connell (who had died in the previous year). O'Brien, a popular and respected figure in Limerick, attempted to remonstrate with the crowd, but was violently attacked and struck in the face by a stone. His face disfigured and his pride badly shaken, O'Brien considered withdrawing completely from public life. He only returned to the Confederation on condition that Mitchel resign, which he did on 3 May.[24]

In quieter times the government might have chosen to ignore Mitchel's violent rhetoric, but with revolution spreading across Europe and Chartism appearing formidable at home, they were becoming increasingly anxious. Military reinforcements were sent to Dublin, and at the end of March Clarendon decided to act firmly against seditious speeches and newspaper articles. But since sedition was classified as a misdemeanour rather than a felony, conviction usually carried only a short term in prison and was often little deterrent. The government decided therefore to draw up a new bill making treasonable incitement a felony, subject to much heavier penalties, and a Treason-Felony Act was rapidly drafted and rushed through parliament, receiving the royal assent on 22 April. The act would become one of the government's main weapons in combating militant Irish nationalism, and the term 'treason-felon' entered the Irish nationalist lexicon. Clarendon decided to drop the lesser charge of seditious libel against Mitchel and to experiment with prosecuting him under the new act.[25] On 13 May 1848 he was arrested at his home at 8 Ontario Terrace and committed to Newgate prison.

The trials of O'Brien and Meagher for sedition went ahead on 15 and 16 May; both were acquitted as their juries were unable to agree on a verdict. British opinion was scathingly critical of their acquittal and claimed that trial by jury in Ireland was a farce. The authorities were particularly anxious that Mitchel should not slip though the net and took great care to exclude Catholics and repeal sympathisers from his jury. Mitchel was tried in a crowded Green Street courthouse on 25 May. As evidence of his treason, the prosecution cited numerous articles from the *United Irishman* advocating armed insurrection. To link his trial with the republican struggles of the past, Mitchel chose as his defence counsel Robert Holmes, a former United Irishman and brother-in-law of Robert Emmet. The 82-year-old Holmes made a moving speech for the defence that detailed Ireland's past and present grievances but made no real attempt to refute the prosecution charges. Mitchel, however, was well pleased with Holmes's defence, believing it had clearly established that his life was another 'link in the unbroken chain of testimony borne by my country against foreign dominion; and with this consciousness I knew that my chains would weigh light'. After two days the jury retired for three hours and delivered a verdict of guilty that evening. Sentence was postponed to the following day.[26]

That night Dublin was described as being like a city on the eve of insurrection. People had a distracted air, carriages dashed constantly to and from barracks, and troops patrolled the streets. The fearful atmosphere was stoked by handbills that circulated warning jurors that if they convicted Mitchel, 'the blood of that innocent Man of Truth, John Mitchel, [will] be on you and yours, to all eternity' and 'the fate of perjurers and assassins awaits you'.[27] Many rank-and-file Confederates spoke of mounting a rescue attempt, and that evening several hundred members of the Dublin clubs marched by Newgate in military formation. But the prison was well guarded, and the Confederate leadership believed that their ill-armed forces could do little and ordered that no attempt should be made. Mitchel was deeply disappointed by their decision. When a Confederate delegation called on him and asked him to sign an address to the clubs forbidding a rescue attempt, he was contemptuous of his colleagues' timidity and, as he later put it, 'refused utterly; and perhaps too bitterly'. Young Dublin Confederates such as John O'Leary and John Savage, who later became prominent Fenians, were also bitterly angry to see their 'foremost man' left to suffer his fate without a struggle.[28]

The following day Mitchel was sentenced to fourteen years' transportation, a sentence that shocked most observers by its severity. Mitchel, though, expressed himself well satisfied. It had been his intention all along to provoke the government to convict him by a packed jury to demonstrate that the rule of law did not apply in Ireland. His speech from the dock was unrepentant: 'I do not regret anything that I have done, and I believe that the course which I have opened is only commenced.' His final words sparked a dramatic courtroom scene: 'The Roman who saw his hand burning to ashes before the tyrant promised that three hundred should follow out his enterprises. Can I not promise for one (he pointed at Meagher) – for two (at Reilly) – for three (at Martin) – aye for hundreds?' There were loud cheers of support and a rush of outstretched hands towards the dock as the judges withdrew in disorder and Mitchel was bundled out of the court.[29]

He was allowed to see his wife and two eldest sons briefly in his cell, and was then taken in chains under a strong escort of dragoons to the steamship, the *Shearwater*, on the North Wall. Sailing from Dublin Bay, he gazed ruefully upon a 'city of bellowing slaves – villas of genteel dastards' and wondered what would become of his wife and five young children. The *Shearwater* took him to Spike Island, and on 1 June he was placed aboard a large war steamer, the *Scourge*, and sailed for Bermuda.[30]

British establishment opinion, characterised by the *Times*, congratulated itself that justice had been done. Mitchel, it claimed, was 'guilty of horrors surpassing the accumulative crimes of all the convicts in Australia . . . He has courted his fate. Let him have it.' Only a 'taint of madness in his character' could explain his conduct. *Punch* magazine famously caricatured him as a pike-wielding monkey, daring to threaten the majesty and power of the British lion. For the British establishment he was the epitome of the incorrigible Celt – a vitriol-flinging, hate-filled fanatic, impossible to satisfy and impervious to reason. [31]

For nationalist Ireland, however, Mitchel's martyrdom created a mood of fierce resentment against the government, and membership of the Confederate clubs doubled after his sentence. Protest meetings were held in Dublin and by Chartists in Lancashire: 15,000 demonstrated at Oldham to express their outrage. Under the sentence of treason-felony, Mitchel lost all title to his property, which was seized by the state; as a result, his family were left destitute, but a public subscription for them soon raised £2,000. Mitchel became a unifying symbol for nationalists and aroused great sympathy even among those who found his beliefs repugnant. Observers such as the Celtic scholar John O'Donovan who had regarded him as a blustering crank – 'he had no party in this kingdom able to dethrone a cat' – were won over by his defiant and dignified bearing before the court: 'I never believed him honest till the last day of his trial, but then saw clearly that he was a second Emmet.'[32]

CHAPTER 4

In Exile, 1848-53

The crew of the *Scourge* had been given instructions to treat Mitchel well on his voyage into exile: he was given a well-furnished two-roomed cabin, allowed exercise on deck, and took his meals with the ship's officers. Mitchel thought it a typical example of British hypocrisy to convict him as a felon and treat him as a gentleman, but he kept his political harangues to himself and stayed on friendly terms with the ship's officers, several of whom lent him books. On 20 June he sighted Bermuda for the first time. There was no actual convict settlement on the island; instead convicts were housed in a number of large prison ships (hulks) just off the coast and worked as labourers on the naval works. On learning that he was to be housed in the convict hulk *Dromedary*, Mitchel noted: 'No sea-side cottages or cedar valleys for me – *à l'outrance*, then, Gaffer Bull.' But compared with the other prisoners Mitchel was in a privileged position: he was treated with respect by the guards, allowed wear his own clothes, and was not given any work to do. He was also kept apart from ordinary convicts – it seems the authorities believed that he might incite mutiny among the prisoners. But he was close enough to recoil at their 'brutal obscenity and stupid blasphemy' and to hear their screams when they were flogged. Although in principle he was not opposed to flogging, in practice he found that he preferred to be out of hearing 'when even felons are getting mangled'.[1]

Although his conditions were not too uncomfortable, he pined for his family and realised that 'Long years in a lonely dungeon are no light thing to the stoutest heart – not to be laughed at by any means.' He contemplated suicide, which he believed was 'not in itself a bad act', but decided against it because of his duty to his family and the belief that he was a far greater irritant to the British Empire alive than dead. He concluded that captivity and suffering are 'nothing to a man unless they *conquer* him and they shall not conquer me – I often say to myself many a better man has been starved to death'.[2]

Although he was forbidden to read any political material or newspapers, occasionally a sympathetic guard smuggled one in to him. News reached him that John Martin and Thomas Devin Reilly had started a newspaper, the *Irish Felon*, to carry on his work. Towards the end of August he learned that warrants had been issued for the arrest of several leading Confederates, and that some, including Martin, had already been imprisoned. All the militant nationalist newspapers, including the *Felon*, had been suppressed. Mitchel was encouraged: 'In short, everything goes on in the genuine '98 style. I like all this very well.' The severity of Mitchel's sentence had helped to steel the resolve of the Confederate leaders, who on the morning after his deportation had formally resolved upon a rising. After *habeas corpus* was suspended on 25 July, leading Confederates attempted to mount an insurrection in Counties Kilkenny and Tipperary, but their poorly prepared efforts soon fizzled out in the face of popular apathy and clerical opposition. Mitchel termed their attempt 'a poor extemporised abortion of a rising' and was critical of its leaders' planning: 'No rising must begin in the country. Dublin streets for that.'[3]

Mitchel whiled away the long hours in his cell by reading and keeping a journal. He hoped it would be a record for his family in future years and a useful therapeutic outlet for himself: 'A vicious

tirade discharged into this receptacle relieves me much . . . A good
rant, like a canter on the back of a brisk horse, gives me an appetite
for dinner.'[4] With no congenial company to divert him, the journal
allowed him to carry on proxy conversations such as that between
the moderate Doppelganger and the violent Ego:

> *Doppelganger*: . . . I am forced to conclude that your anxiety for the
> success of the French Republic springs from something else than zeal
> for the welfare of the human race.
> *The Ego*: A fig for the human race; to be sure it does.
> *Doppelganger*: Yes; it is born of no love for mankind, or even French
> mankind, but of pure hatred to England, and a diseased longing for
> blood and carnage . . .
> *The Ego*: Go to – the revolutionary Leveller is your only architect . . .
> Wherever you see a greedy tyranny (constitutional or other) grinding
> the faces of the poor, join battle with it on the spot – conspire, confed-
> erate, and combine against it, resting never till the huge mischief come
> down, though the whole 'structure of society' come down along with
> it . . . Courage, Jacobins! for ye, too, are ministers of heaven. . . . I
> prescribe copious blood-letting upon strictly therapeutical principles.[5]

Some years earlier when reviewing a work by the imprisoned
Chartist Thomas Cooper, Mitchel had written: 'To take a man
from the occupations and distractions of everyday life, to place
him in a study where he cannot be disturbed, to drive him to mental
exertion as a necessary pastime, to strengthen his intellect by
discipline and constant application, and to steep his heart in gall
and bitterness, and make it beat only for revenge, appears to be the
maddest mode of checking dangerous opinions, or interfering with
the most effective exertion of men.'[6] So it was with Mitchel: captivity reinforced his hostility to Britain and gave him time to create
his classic memoir of hatred of British rule. There are other hymns

of hate in the Irish nationalist canon, but none composed with the literary virtuosity of Mitchel's *Jail Journal*. In the blink of an eye he can switch from spewing forth venomous hatred of England to ruminating on the beauties of nature. It is, above all, the *Jail Journal*'s combination of violent hatred and poetic sensibility that makes it an affecting and disturbing work at the same time.

For Mitchel, Britain was the embodiment of the hypocrisy of the age, hiding her exploitation and ruthlessness beneath a cloak of benevolence. Her empire was 'a vast, organised imposture; a machine for *exploiting* nations; an unmixed and unredeemed mischief, whose fruits are torture in India, opium in China, famine in Ireland, pauperism in England, disturbance and disorder in Europe, and robbery everywhere'.[7] Yet despite the British Empire's great power, Mitchel believed that it was already in serious decline. His usual derisory term for Britain was 'Carthage', a commercial empire dominated by speculators and stockjobbers, so obsessed with making money that it was fast losing its martial spirit and like the Carthage of old would one day be destroyed: 'British policy must drain the blood and suck the marrow of all the nations it can fasten its desperate claws upon: and by the very nature of a bankrupt concern sustaining itself on false credit, its exertions must grow more desperate, its exactions more ruthless day by day, until the mighty smash come.'[8]

Such a collapse corresponded with Mitchel's view of history. He dismissed as self-congratulatory propaganda the grand historical narratives of the nineteenth century, such as Macaulay's *History of England*, which traced the onward march of human progress and perfectibility. In opposition to such Whiggish optimism, Mitchel took a cyclical rather than a linear view of history, maintaining that the powerful would inevitably one day be brought to earth, and that their place would be taken by nations which were now weak or oppressed. But they too in turn would repeat 'the same crimes and suffer the same penalties. For the progress of the species is circular.'[9]

Mitchel believed that notions of moral or social progress were illusory, and he was contemptuous of the smug and self-satisfied spirit of his day. He dismissed the widely held belief that the nineteenth century was the pinnacle of human achievement, and believed that its self-glorification simply indicated its shallowness and stupidity. Instead he claimed that 'The happiest, the best social system that has yet existed was the earliest and the simplest. Many wise men have held that as society grew in years and ages, it grew in vice: that the more advanced we get in civilisation, the worse and more depraved we get and that is all.'[10]

Like his mentor Carlyle, Mitchel tended to exaggerate contemporary celebration of material progress in order to portray himself as a lone voice daring to cry out against the materialism and complacency of the Victorian age. He relished ridiculing the benefits of technological progress: 'If a man tell a lie at one end of a wire, it will not come out truth at the other end. The railroad carries men very quickly upon their business, such as it is, be their errands good or evil, be their intents wicked or charitable.'[11] Contrasting the nineteenth century's concern with physical comfort with the ideals of the ancient Greeks, he noted that they at least regarded 'truth, fortitude, honesty, purity, as the great objects of human effort, and *not* the supply of vulgar wants'. Not surprisingly, he reserved his greatest contempt for Britain, the country in which technological progress was most advanced, and scoffed at events such as the Great Exhibition of 1851, in which a purpose-built palace was filled to the brim with the latest gadgets and proclaimed as evidence of Britain's mastery of the world. His hatred of material progress and hatred of Britain went hand in hand – each feeding off the other.[12] But Mitchel was adamant that he hated the British imperial system rather than its common people, whom he described as 'voteless, landless, rightless, who labour for ever in mines and factories, who have no part in the government of their own land, no interest in the oppression of Ireland, in the plunder of Asia, or in the European balance of power'. He claimed that in seeking to overthrow a system that so ruthlessly exploited the poor, he was in fact being a friend to ordinary Britons.[13]

Towards the end of September 1848 Mitchel was afflicted with a severe bout of asthma that lasted over two months. He cursed Bermuda's intense humidity and its damp and piercing winds. He could not sleep at nights, and he grew thin and weak. Reading brought little relief: 'Enough of books – I would give all the books I ever read for a pair of lungs that would work.' The prison doctor told him that he would die if kept in Bermuda much longer, and persuaded him to write to the governor requesting a transfer to another colony with a drier climate. Mitchel was deeply reluctant to ask the authorities for anything but, although it cost him 'a grievous effort', he eventually did so.[14]

In February 1849 he learned that he was to be transferred to the Cape of Good Hope, and on 22 April he and several hundred other prisoners (200 of them Irish) boarded the *Neptune*, a large sailing ship, and set out for the Cape. The voyage was expected to take about two months, but it was beset by contrary winds and after three months there was still no sight of land. Food and water rations were cut to half for crew and prisoners; many were ill with scurvy, and seven died. The ship's parson confided in Mitchel that 'We shall have mutiny here . . . We shall have murder, and canni-balism, and everything horrible.' Mitchel replied that 'in Ireland people had been eating each other for some time, though lean – and I eyed his well-filled waistcoat. He shuddered visibly: said he trusted it would all end well.'[15]

On 20 July 1849 they put ashore at the Brazilian port of Pernambuco (Recife) to take on fresh supplies. The *Neptune*

resumed its journey on 10 August and arrived at the Cape on 19
September. Its arrival sparked a serious political controversy. The
Cape's inhabitants, three quarters of them Dutch, had earlier
received assurances that their colony would receive no more
convicts, and had formed an Anti-Convict Association. With the
arrival of the *Neptune* their agitation reached a pitch, and they
pledged to resist the landing of any convicts. Mitchel was highly
amused by the authorities' difficulties, and although his health had
suffered during the long voyage and he longed to walk on dry land
again, he reckoned his discomfort was a small price to pay for the
British government's embarrassment. He was particularly encouraged that the Boers – self-reliant farmers with 'a wholesome taste
for powder and ball' – were willing to resist their imperial masters by
force of arms if necessary. He predicted that London's arrogance
would transform Dutch and English settlers 'into a self-dependent,
high-spirited nation of South Africans', and he toasted 'in red wine
of Cape vines, the health of the future South African Republic'.[16]

The Boers held firm, and the protest continued for six months.
Finally the government relented, and on 19 February 1850 the
Neptune, with its cargo of convicts, left the Cape for Van Diemen's
Land, docking at Hobart on 7 April. Because of the hardship they
had suffered since leaving Bermuda, the *Neptune*'s convicts were to
be set free on Van Diemen's Land. This stipulation did not apply to
Mitchel, but he was offered and accepted a 'ticket-of-leave' which
allowed him to travel as he pleased within his resident police district
once he had given his parole not to escape and reported monthly to
the local police magistrate. Mitchel, as ever, was uneasy about
accepting any indulgence from the authorities, but his health was
shattered after a full year at sea and he believed it was the only way
to save his life.[17] All the other Young Ireland prisoners who had been
sent to the island, except O'Brien, had done the same. Although a
political prisoner was not normally allowed choose a district where

another political prisoner resided, this rule was relaxed for Mitchel because he was so ill that he needed someone to take care of him. He was to live with John Martin (transported the previous summer) at Bothwell, a quiet village 46 miles inland from Hobart.

Martin was immediately struck by Mitchel's poor health, but noted that his old fieriness had not waned: 'He is in great spirits and as fierce as ten lions, and bullies me outrageously.' He arranged for Mitchel to meet the other Young Ireland prisoners, Meagher and Kevin Izod O'Doherty, at Lake Sorel, where their various police districts converged. This was illegal under the terms of their ticket-of-leave, but the authorities generally paid little heed to whatever happened outside the main towns. The lake was several hours' ride from Bothwell, and it took its toll on Mitchel's fragile health. Meagher was astonished at how Mitchel had deteriorated in the last two years, and thought he was on the verge of death: 'His worn and sunken cheeks, his dull blood-shot eyes, his moist hand, his thick and gasping articulation, his stooped shoulders, his slow and undecided step – everything about him filled me with the saddest apprehension.' The old friends greeted each other with 'hearty, vociferous and spontaneous' laughter, but after talking of events in Ireland and the factionalism of Irish political refugees in America, their meeting soon 'grew dismal enough'.[18]

Meagher's fears for Mitchel proved unfounded, and over the next few weeks, with Martin's care, the pleasant climate and regular exercise, his health improved rapidly. After two years on board various ships, much of it in near-solitary confinement, he enjoyed the pleasures of walking on *terra firma* and haranguing Martin. His health quickly improved, and soon he was riding up to forty miles a day, leaping fences and walking long distances.[19] At first Mitchel did not want his family to join him, fearful of exposing them to 'the felonious atmosphere' of Tasmania. But he missed them greatly and eventually persuaded himself that by living on an isolated farm he could protect his children from any corrupting influences; the climate and fresh air would be good for them, and he would have plenty of time to devote to their education. He admitted: 'I do so pine for something resembling a home'; and on 22 July he wrote to his family asking them to come out: 'Pray God, I have done right.'[20]

Almost a year elapsed before they could join him, during which Mitchel often found life rather dull: 'Our main object has been to kill thought by violent exercise on foot and on horseback. We still go to the lakes and meet with Meagher, and this is our chiefest pleasure.' Sometimes he and Martin diverted themselves by hunting kangaroos on horseback, using greyhounds to run down their prey. During the years they would spend together in exile the two men generally got along together well, but Mitchel's moodiness could try even the patience of the saintly Martin, and both men looked forward to the arrival of Mitchel's family.[21]

Mitchel's wife, three sons, John, James and William, and two daughters, Henrietta and Mary, arrived in Hobart on 18 June 1851 and had an emotional reunion with Mitchel two days later. In August 1851 they moved to a new home, Nant Cottage, three miles from Bothwell, with a pasture farm of 200 acres which Mitchel stocked with sheep and cattle. Throughout all his tribulations his family was his greatest source of consolation, and many friends noticed how his wife and children brought out the best in him. He could be reserved or distant with those he did not know well, but was usually at his kindest and most cheerful with his family. Once they had arrived, Mitchel bore his exile with greater equanimity and began to think that perhaps he could serve out his whole sentence and return to Ireland with his family when it was over.[22] Trips to Lake Sorel to meet Meagher and O'Doherty became regular events, and Mitchel and his wife rode out to see O'Brien in October 1851. It was the first time they had met since Mitchel's deportation, and O'Brien still blamed Mitchel for his injuries at Limerick three years earlier. Nevertheless he enjoyed meeting him, noting that 'With many of Mitchel's opinions I wholly disagree, but there is something in the sturdiness of his character that I admire: and as he is an accomplished scholar a day could not be passed in his society without gratification, even by a stranger fond of literary pursuits.'[23] Mitchel had appealing personal qualities that rarely come across in his strident public writings; his private letters are often enlivened by a playful, self-deprecating wit, and many friends who despaired of his extreme beliefs and violent language nonetheless felt great personal warmth towards him. Mitchel fully reciprocated in his admiration for O'Brien, regarding him as 'this noblest of Irishmen', but the two men still found much on which to differ. Deeply disillusioned by the failure of the 1848 insurrection, O'Brien regarded the cause of Irish independence as lost forever, but Mitchel still believed that, in the right circumstances, independence could be wrested from Britain. They discussed this and other matters many times over the next two years, without ever yielding an inch. They often joked that should either of them attain a position of power in an independent Ireland, they would have no choice but to hang the other.[24]

Mitchel's opinion of Tasmania waxed and waned. He thought its forests, mountains and lakes were beautiful, but constantly reminded himself that they were 'but Carthaginian prison walls'. He particularly disliked going to the major towns, which readily reminded him that he was confined to a British penal colony: 'Every sight or sound that strikes eye or ear on this mail road, reminds me that I am in a small misshapen, transported, bastard England; and the legitimate England is not so dear to me that I can love the convict copy.' As he looked at his fellow inhabitants, ploughing or tending flocks, or singing in the fields, 'instead of rejoicing in *their* improved conditions and behaviour, I gaze on them with horror as unclean and inhuman monsters, due long ago to the gallows-tree and oblivion'. Although they were friendly to one another and to travellers, and generally 'comport themselves partly like human beings . . . human they are not. Their training has made them subterhuman, preterhuman; and the system of British "reformatory discipline" has gone as near to making them perfect fiends, as human wit can go.'[25]

A marked pessimism pervaded Mitchel's view of human nature. He did not believe that people were naturally good, or that they were capable of much improvement. He was contemptuous of fashionable philanthropic schemes for rehabilitating criminals and argued that 'Instead of severe, sanguinary, sharp and decisive punishments, which would repress crime, modern philanthropy so pampers and tenderly entreats the criminal as to put a premium on villainy.'[26] 'In criminal jurisprudence,' he noted, 'as well as in many another things, the nineteenth century is sadly retrogressive; and your Beccarias, and Howards, and Romillys are genuine apostles of barbarism.' In a passage that could have come from Carlyle's 'Model Prisons' in his *Latter-day Pamphlets* (1850), Mitchel asked:

> What to do, then, with all our robbers, burglars, and forgers? Why hang them, *hang* them. You have no right to make the honest people support the rogues, and support them better than they, the honest people, can support themselves . . . Jails ought to be places of discomfort; the 'sanitary condition' of miscreants ought not to be better cared for than the honest, industrious people – and for 'ventilation', I would ventilate the rascals in front of the county jails at the end of a rope.[27]

The presence of his family gave Mitchel's life more purpose and variety, and he devoted himself to farming and to educating his children. He had something approaching a normal family life and his wife gave birth to another child, Isabel. But he noted that although 'I have books, companions, fields to till, children to teach, and in fact am busy from morning to night; yet I feel idle, listless, unsatisfied'. He frequently spoke of life in Tasmania as a form of hibernation, a dream-like killing of time, or even a coma.[28] Unable to concentrate, he read little, and stopped making entries in his journal, only breaking a fifteen-month gap on 1 January 1853: 'Of literature I am almost sick, and prefer farming, and making market of my wool. There is somewhat stupefying to the brain, as well as invigorating to the frame, in this genial clime and aromatic air . . . [Martin] and I have eaten narcotic lotus here; and if it has not removed, it has surely softened the sting, even of our *nostalgia* . . . Surely it is not good for us to be here.'[29] In the same month, the receipt of a long letter from Thomas Devin Reilly, who had escaped to America and thrown himself into American politics as a fervent Democrat, sharpened Mitchel's unease. After the heady political excitement he had experienced in Ireland he could never be content with being a sheep farmer in Tasmania.

By this time Meagher and Terence Bellew McManus, another of the Young Irelanders transported in July 1849, had escaped from the island: McManus in the autumn of 1851 and Meagher some months later. By August 1852 Mitchel was already thinking on similar lines.[30] In January 1853 the Young Irelander P. J. Smyth arrived in Tasmania to help the Irish prisoners to escape. Neither O'Brien nor Martin was prepared to do so, but Mitchel was willing, and his wife strongly urged him to go. For months Smyth and Mitchel made escape plans, and finally decided to make the attempt on 9 June. For Mitchel it was particularly important that he should revoke his parole in an honourable manner: he was unhappy that Meagher had done so by post. Mitchel believed that this reflected badly on Meagher's fellow prisoners and the cause of Irish nationalism, and insisted on revoking his parole in person and giving the police some opportunity to seize him.[31]

On 9 June 1853 Mitchel and Smyth, both armed, entered the police station at Bothwell. Mitchel handed the police magistrate a note withdrawing his parole and offering himself to be taken into custody. While the magistrate read the note, Smyth's hand rested on a revolver in his coat and Mitchel clutched a heavy riding whip. The police officials present seemed stupefied and only reacted when the two turned on their heels and left the station. Mitchel and Smyth immediately mounted their horses (which were being held by a constable) and rode off at speed. The magistrate rushed out into the street, ordering passers-by to stop them. But most Tasmanians had little sympathy for the authorities, and nobody made any effort to intervene or hide their amusement as the fugitives galloped away.[32]

Once outside Bothwell, Mitchel and Smyth separated, Mitchel going north. For the next six weeks a series of misadventures prevented him from getting off the island, but while in hiding he was sheltered and received such generous help from the local inhabitants, of Irish, Scottish and English origins, that he easily evaded the police's half-hearted efforts to arrest him. On 12 July Mitchel travelled to Hobart disguised as a Catholic priest, and a week later, with the help of a sympathetic ship's captain, sailed to Sydney, arriving on 23 July. On 1 August he took the first available ship for Tahiti, where on 13 September he was joined by his family, and together they boarded the *Julia Ann*, an American schooner. Once aboard, Mitchel doffed his hat to the Stars and Stripes and congratulated himself on being a free man again.[33]

CHAPTER 5

Liberty in America, 1853-4

On 9 October 1853 the *Julia Ann* arrived in San Francisco. Mitchel was greeted by Terence Bellew McManus, who had settled in California after his escape, and on 26 October was honoured by a grand banquet presided over by the state governor. After three weeks of celebrations he observed: 'I am for the moment a great man, but I am glad we run off so soon, lest the people might find me out.' He liked California and was tempted to settle there, but believed he could do more for Irish nationalism in New York. With this in mind, he travelled east and arrived in New York with his family on 29 November 1853. He received an enthusiastic welcome: a large crowd cheered him at the harbour, bands played, militia companies with fixed bayonets lined the streets, and the Napper Tandy Light Artillery gave him a 31-gun salute. The welcoming party included Meagher and Mitchel's brother William, who had emigrated from Ireland in 1848. They took the family to Union Street, Brooklyn, to join Mitchel's mother and sister, who had moved there during his captivity. The Mitchel home soon became a magnet for old friends and fellow exiles such as John Blake Dillon, his wife Adelaide, Richard O'Gorman and Michael Doheny.[1]

Mitchel's first impressions of New York were of a frenetically busy city. He found the pace of life so fast that at times he longed for the peace and tranquillity of Tasmania. Again he found himself fêted. Deputations from societies, clubs, and volunteer companies called to his home, and there was much handshaking and speech making. Mitchel thought it all 'very absurd', but after his years in prison and exile he enjoyed the attention. He was also given a civic reception in City Hall, and used the opportunity to berate bitterly the British government, which made his hosts rather uneasy. With war about to break out between Russia and England, Mitchel was rather taken aback by the largely pro–British sympathies of much of the American public and press, and resolved to counter this by publishing a weekly paper aimed at the Irish-American community. Called the *Citizen*, it was first published on 7 January 1854 and sold well.[2]

In the *Citizen* Mitchel called for the creation of an Irish organisation to take advantage of British difficulties. The led to the founding of the Irishmen's Civil and Military Republican Union in New York in April 1854, but it soon collapsed. Its main significance was that it was replaced in early 1855 by the Emmet Monument Association, which in turn acted as a precursor to the Fenian Brotherhood founded in 1858.[3] Mitchel also travelled to Washington to seek aid for Ireland from the Russian ambassador. The ambassador was a regular reader of the *Citizen* and well aware of Mitchel's hatred for Britain, but he made it clear that as Russia's ships were blockaded there was no practical way for Russia to assist the Irish cause. At first Mitchel had thought that the war would spread beyond the Black Sea and the Baltic, but when it seemed that it would be largely confined to these theatres, and that there was nothing that Russia could do to aid an Irish insurrection, he largely lost interest.[4]

He continued, nevertheless, to hope for a great European war. While most nineteenth-century liberals deprecated war, priding themselves on living in an age of peace and progress, Mitchel rejoiced in it, claiming that through war nations gained strength and vitality. He was exhilarated on hearing of the outbreak of the

Crimean War: 'I believe in moral and spiritual electricity; I believe that a spark, caught at some happy moment, may give life to masses of comatose humanity . . . Give us war in our time, O Lord!' [5] He maintained that

> Peace indeed is sometimes beautiful, but is often ignoble corrupt and ignominious. Not peace but war has called forth the grandest, finest, tenderest, most generous qualities of manhood and womanhood . . . War is as needful to agitate and purify the moral atmosphere as thunderstorms to stir and cleanse the material air we breathe . . . Let wars be miraculously abolished and the 'canker of long peace' will kill the soul of nations and of men; in the foul air of that corruption will grow monsters enough and the progress of the species will be backward indeed.[6]

He scorned the optimism of liberals such as John Bright and Richard Cobden who believed that international commerce was a civilising force which would bind nations together, and thus make war impossible. To Mitchel the nineteenth-century *Pax Britannica* was a fraud that allowed Britain to dominate the globe through her trade and commerce. He argued that commerce had 'nothing elevating, refining or purifying in it' but was in fact a heartless force that destroyed more innocent people than any war, its victims 'more miserably and ignominiously slain than war at its worst and wickedest could ever slay'.[7]

Mitchel's arrival in New York coincided with the growth of nativism as a powerful political force in America. As increasing numbers of foreigners, especially poor Irish Catholics, arrived in America, the nativists or 'Know-Nothings' claimed that American Protestants would be swamped and American liberties subverted by papist intolerance. There were frequent violent clashes between nativists and Catholics, and several Catholic churches were wrecked. One of Mitchel's reasons for publishing the *Citizen* was to defend the Irish from nativist attacks, and he regularly poured scorn on exaggerated Protestant fears of Jesuit conspiracies and papal inquisitions. He equated 'Know-Nothings' with abolitionists, both of whom largely drew their adherents from Protestant evangelicals. Almost from its beginning the *Citizen* was engaged in bitter controversy with the abolitionist movement, triggered by a letter from the Dublin Quaker James Haughton to Meagher, demanding that Young Ireland exiles in New York should explicitly condemn slavery. While working for the *Nation*, Mitchel, already sympathetic to American slaveholders, was exasperated by the calls of Haughton and others to denounce slavery. Gavan Duffy maintained that in 1846–7 he had to censor several of Mitchel's articles in the *Nation* attacking abolitionism and the emancipation of the Jews. Most Young Irelanders opposed slavery but were anxious to avoid entanglement in a bitter controversy that would distract them from Irish matters. Daniel O'Connell, however, considered slavery such a great evil that he missed no opportunity to condemn it, and he refused to accept donations from American slaveholders, declaring that he wanted 'no American aid if it comes across the Atlantic stained in Negro blood'. Mitchel believed that tensions over slavery between O'Connell and the Young Irelanders had contributed to the secession of July 1846.[8]

Never one to respond well to preaching, Mitchel rounded on Haughton, contrasting his concern for the sufferings of Africans with his alleged indifference to the sufferings of his own countrymen during the Famine. Mitchel stated his position clearly:

> We are not abolitionists: no more abolitionists than Moses or Socrates or Jesus Christ. We deny that it is a crime, or a wrong, or even a peccadillo, to hold slaves, to buy slaves, to keep slaves to their work by flogging or other needful coercion . . . and as for being a participator in the wrongs, we, for our part, wish we had a good plantation, well-stocked with healthy negroes, in Alabama.[9]

This last remark became one of his most notorious, and he was roundly condemned by abolitionists 'as a curse to the soil on which he treads, and a poison to the atmosphere which he breathes'. A leading abolitionist, the Rev. Henry Ward Beecher (brother of Harriet Beecher Stowe, the author of *Uncle Tom's Cabin*), denounced him as a hypocrite who supported liberty in Ireland but advocated slavery in America. The more he was denounced the more vigorously Mitchel defended slavery. In reply to Beecher, he observed that his view was merely that of 'the legislators of the Jews, and the wise men of the Greeks and the framers of the Declaration of Independence' and he reiterated: 'My position was and is the naked assertion "that slaveholding is not a crime" and that nobody ever thought it a crime until some time towards the close of the last century.'[10]

Many of Mitchel's friends were shocked and tried to persuade him to soften his tone, but he would not retract a word, continuing to argue that slavery 'is good in itself, good in its relations with other countries, good in every way'. Mitchel maintained that a society based on free competition resulted in the exploitation of the weak, whereas the slave system provided for the social well-being of all. Under capitalism, employer and employee were linked only by the degrading cash nexus, but the slaveowner had stronger obligations to care for the welfare of his slaves. As on other issues, Mitchel echoed Carlyle. In his *Occasional Discourse on the Negro Question* (1849), Carlyle had supported slavery on the basis that negroes were born to be mastered. Similarly, Mitchel was unashamedly racist in his reasoning: he argued that blacks were an innately inferior people who lived in a state of barbarism in Africa, and that 'to enslave them is impossible, or to set them free either; they are born and bred slaves'.[11] He claimed that it was right to go to Africa, where most of the population were already enslaved by 'ignorant and brutal negroes', and to buy there as many slaves as possible so they could be raised 'out of the most miserable and abject of all possible human conditions, to the comparative happiness and dignity of plantation hands. This is right, just and humane. The more slaves from Africa, the better *for the slaves*.'[12]

Mitchel enjoyed provoking and outraging abolitionists, regarding them as the embodiment of the hypocrisy of the age. He despised their Calvinist self-righteousness, ridiculed their belief in human improvement, and lumped together as crackpot crusades their advocacy of pacifism, vegetarianism, women's rights, penal reform, and the abolition of capital punishment. He attacked their tightly circumscribed ideas of philanthropy, claiming that all their concern was directed towards negro slaves, while they were blind to the sufferings of poor whites in their midst. These were the very people who ascribed the starvation of millions in Ireland to the designs of Providence, or who, through the heartless gospel of *laissez-faire*, worked the factory hands of Manchester and New York into early graves. American abolitionists were, moreover, dupes of the British government which had encouraged their agitation to foment disorder in the United States and weaken a rival power.[13]

Mitchel scoffed at the high-blown rhetoric used by abolitionists: 'Men have no business to speculate about "destinies" and "missions", but should just do the best they can in their generation.' He taunted Beecher with his habit of uttering 'kind-looking sentences' and 'prevailing cants', and assuming 'the credit of benevolence, and philanthropy, and enlightenment, and "progress" and all the rest of it'. He claimed that the so-called Enlightenment of the eighteenth century had introduced a new era of hypocrisy and he dismissed many of the Enlightenment's fundamental ideals. Confronted by an abolitionist with the opening lines of the American Declaration of Independence, Mitchel retorted: 'I am not aware that every human being, or any one, has "an inalienable right to life, liberty, and happiness". People often forfeit life and liberty, and as to "happiness" I do not even know what it is. On the whole, I fear this is jargon.'[14]

Although Mitchel's views on slavery infuriated northern abolitionists, they were warmly received in the South, and in June 1854 he was invited to give the annual graduation day speech at the University of Virginia at Charlottesville. He used the opportunity to attack aggressive modernity and technology worship, maintaining that the nineteenth century's confidence in material progress and human improvement was deeply mistaken. Even in the agrarian South Mitchel's views were regarded as reactionary, and greeted with restrained applause, but nevertheless he enjoyed his visit: he thought Virginia beautiful, and was delighted by the charm and kindness of the people. On his return to New York, however, he soon found himself in the teeth of another controversy.

The city's Catholic archbishop, John Hughes, perceiving some anticlerical tendencies in the exiled Young Irelanders, had dismissed them as an unrepresentative group, 'distrusted and scorned' by their fellow Irishmen. Mitchel responded with a scathing attack on 'the treachery and meanness of the Irish Catholic priests' and denounced Hughes's support for the overthrow of the Roman Republic in 1849. He claimed that the pope was 'a bad prince and his government a mischievous government', and that Hughes and his fellow clergy were 'bad republicans' who abused the toleration granted them by the American constitution. Hughes, a former labourer, was not averse to bare-knuckle polemics himself and responded in kind. He denounced Mitchel as a 'vitriol flinger' and an 'apologist of the scurvy tricks' of the Young Irelanders and taunted him that he was 'intended by the circumstances of nativity and neighbourhood, to be a mere sturdy Orangeman of the North'. This provoked Mitchel to even greater vituperation, and he described Hughes as 'an unworthy prelate' and 'an ally of the Know-Nothings'. The hierarchy and priests were 'an enemy to

Irishmen – they betrayed their own people in '98 and '48; no terms are to be kept with such inveterate and treacherous enemies. If the freedom of Ireland is ever to be won, it must be won in spite of the priests.'[15] The controversy was more a clash of personalities than principles, but many New York Catholics were appalled at Mitchel's tone towards their clergy, and the *Citizen* lost thousands of readers. Years later Mitchel admitted that he had gone too far: 'I am not patient of ecclesiastical censure; and replied perhaps too bitterly; and more than once . . . I would if I could erase from the page and from all men's memory, about three-fourths of what I then wrote and published.'[16]

By now he was disillusioned with New York, having sacrificed his popularity through his taste for controversy. He also had a problem with his eyesight and was advised by his doctors to give up journalism for a while. At the end of 1854 he signed the *Citizen* over to a colleague and decided to leave New York.

CHAPTER 6

Southern Citizen, 1855-65

After a year of bitter controversies Mitchel was feeling at his most misanthropic and wished to settle somewhere remote from human society. Since he had been received with hospitality and respect on his visits to the South and had enjoyed its slower pace of life, he decided to settle there. He chose eastern Tennessee, where he was told that the countryside was beautiful and the land cheap. In March 1855 he left New York with his family and travelled to Knoxville, east Tennessee. He spent some weeks exploring the surrounding country, hoping to find somewhere 'beyond the barking of dogs, and the advertisements of town lots and Cherry Pectoral'. Lamenting the spread of civilisation, he noted 'that one is inclined to remonstrate at having been introduced to the earth at so late a date'.[1] Eventually he heard of a beautiful valley called Tucaleechee Cove, high up in the Allegheny mountains, about 35 miles from Knoxville. On his first visit Mitchel was taken by its seclusion and beauty, and bought a 140-acre farm, moving there with his family at the end of May. There was much work to do in putting the farm and its dilapidated log cabin in order, and his neighbours helped out. He found them 'excessively ignorant and cunning, but civil', and he admired their robust egalitarianism and self-reliance. Mitchel recorded a typical evening with his neighbours as they sat around the cabin fire smoking and talking. Most of them had seen little of the world and were fascinated by

this much-travelled stranger; they asked if it was true that sea
water was salty. Mitchel's confirmation that this was indeed the
case was greeted with their habitual exclamation of 'Wall, I do
wonder!'[2]

Many such remote regions were touched by evangelical 'awake-
nings' during the 1850s, and one evening Mitchel came across an
outdoor religious meeting. He was appalled by the frenzied ranting
of the preachers and the hysterical weeping and shrieking of the
congregation: 'I entertain a strong repugnance against witnessing
human nature reduced to insane grovelling.'[3] In terms of his
personal beliefs, Mitchel was largely indifferent to religion: he had
a generalised belief in a god, but usually described himself as 'an
unworthy member of the pagan persuasion'. He favoured a clear
distinction between the spiritual and the civil spheres and believed
that once someone obeyed the law, 'he is at liberty to obey also a
Pope in Italy, a Grand Lama in Tartery [*sic*], and everybody else he
pleases'. However, he often displayed a marked sympathy for
Catholicism: when two of his daughters later converted to
Catholicism he offered no opposition, but regarded their action
with benign neutrality as an exercise of private judgement, wryly
admitting: 'There is a kind of hankering in all our family after the
"errors of Romanism".'[4] In political terms, Mitchel believed that
Catholicism was a vital element of Irish nationality that set the
country apart from the Protestant ethos of British imperialism. He
also regarded the Catholic Church as a barrier to aggressive
modernity, praising the papacy's refusal to conform to 'liberalism,
progress and modern civilisation' and rejoicing that 'there is one
power or influence in this world which bids us refuse to bow the
knee to that whore who calls herself the spirit of the age'.[5]

Mitchel, though, had a strong distaste for religious enthusiasm,
particularly for evangelical Protestantism. 'There is plenty of
ignorant papistry', he wrote, 'in Italy and Spain, but Lord bless

you! It is nothing to the benighted Protestantism that runs rampant here in the United States.' He characterised its adherents as 'sickly-looking thin men and grim, meagre hard women of dismal intelligence – for intelligent they are, clear-eyed, high-browed, petrific to gods and men'. When living in Knoxville he attended the local Presbyterian church every Sunday, finding it marginally preferable to the 'horrible noises' that emerged from the nearby revivalist Methodist chapel, but admitted: 'There is no sect of Christians whom I might not be tempted to persecute, if I were in power, for their cup of balderdash is nearly full: except, however, for the present, the Catholic Church.'[6] But although he rejected the religious beliefs of his Dissenting background, he remained strongly influenced by it, his vigorous polemical style owing much to its biblical language and cadences.

Mitchel enjoyed the rugged beauty of Tucaleechee Cove and hunted game with his sons in the well-stocked woods adjoining his farm. Farming kept him occupied, but it did not pay very well, and he had to supplement his income with occasional lecture tours. By the spring of 1856 he was again thinking of moving. His wife had never taken to life in the woods, and by now both were worried about the educational and social disadvantages to their children. They decided to move to Knoxville, where they had a new house built just outside the town, although the move did not take place until September. In this prosperous town of five thousand people Mitchel made some good friends, including the town's mayor, William Swan.

That winter he undertook a lecture tour, visiting several major northern and southern cities, and did so again in January 1858. He believed that most people came to see him just out of curiosity and that 'they would come just as well if I advertised that on a certain evening I would appear upon a platform and stand upon my head there. This is a humiliating reflection to an illustrious patriot, but it can't be helped.' He regarded lecturing as 'a loathsome business which I thought I had renounced for ever; but I want money, and can only think of preying on the public'.[7] These lectures also had a strong political purpose: they were usually strong attacks on the British government's actions in Ireland or abroad, and during the revolt of the Indian army (1857–8) he strongly denounced Britain's 'odious and predatory' imperialism, claiming it had invented sepoy atrocities to justify its own continued cruelties in India. Local newspapers praised his 'mingled bursts of philosophy and poetry' and his 'impassioned eloquence', but Mitchel realised that his anti-British sentiments rarely hit home, the South feeling too well disposed towards its best cotton-buying customer.[8]

Mitchel's lecture tours through the cotton states enabled him to see at first hand the social system he had admired from afar. He concluded that the United States comprised two nations, separated 'by their institutions, habits, industrial requirements and political principles', and that in any conflict his sympathies would be with the South.[9] Conversations with Southern planters as he sailed down the Mississippi reinforced his belief that slavery benefited both master and slave: 'In short, the cause of negro slavery is the cause of true philanthropy, so far as that race is concerned.'[10] Mitchel held to this belief with absolute consistency. When, towards the end of the civil war, the Confederate government proposed to offer slaves freedom in return for fighting for the South, Mitchel was staunchly opposed, arguing that if freedom was a good thing for slaves, then the South had been in the wrong from the start.[11]

In October 1857 he and his friend Swan decided to start a newspaper together to champion slavery. Called the *Southern Citizen*, it would defend the doctrine of states' rights, promote 'the value and virtue of slavery, both for negroes and white men', argue for a reopening of the African slave trade, and encourage the spread of slavery into the new territories of the United States.[12] It also concerned itself with Irish issues, publishing a series of letters to Congressman Alexander Hamilton Stephens of Georgia, later Confederate vice-president, detailing the political history of Ireland during the 1840s and arguing that the British government had exploited the Famine to subjugate Ireland. In 1861 these were collected and published in book form as *The Last Conquest of Ireland (Perhaps)*.

Mitchel took up the fight for slavery with such vehemence that he admitted that 'a great part of the South (besides the whole North) think me mad'.[13] His extreme pro-slavery advocacy was not always welcomed by Southerners, many of whom thought it excessive and playing into the hands of the abolitionists. One Southern paper rebuked him as a self-publicist and 'impertinent foreign meddler' whose 'ability and boldness seems to surpass his discretion and modesty', and claimed that 'he now vapours and struts as if the whole South belonged to him'.[14] A series of attacks on Mitchel published in the Knoxville *Register* in September 1857 so irritated him that he confronted the paper's editor, John Fleming, in a Knoxville street and assaulted him with an ornamental cane, striking him repeatedly with such force that the cane broke. Fleming drew a pistol to defend himself, but the police intervened before anything further could happen. The two men only narrowly avoided fighting a duel afterwards.[15]

Mitchel's extremism appalled many of his friends, and caused John Martin to lose confidence in him as a leader and unifying force for Irish nationalists. Martin deplored his 'haughty violence' and 'wrong-headedness' and wrote telling him so. Mitchel admitted that most of his friends considered him 'either crazy or depraved', but he had no intention of changing, and as for Martin's lectures, 'he might as well whistle jigs to a milestone'. Clearly, though, there was a cooling in their friendship around this time. Mitchel wrote that Martin 'thinks I have been a sort of evil genius to him, feels himself somewhat blackened by my Alabama negros, blushes at my red republicanism, abhors and stigmatises my vitriol, and repudiates my "suicide" and "metempsychosis" . . . What is worse, he thinks some passages in my journal contain some sort of sneer at him.'[16]

Much of Mitchel's affection for the South stemmed from the fact that he saw it as an Arcadian haven from the heartless industrial capitalism that he despised. He argued that North and South were two nations with incompatible social systems drifting wider apart with each passing year, and that the South must finally secede. 'I prefer the South in every sense,' he wrote. 'I do really believe its state of society to be more sound, more just, than that of the North.'[17] He believed that the South, a largely agrarian and slave-holding society whose citizens were self-reliant and well used to arms, was the nineteenth-century polity closest to the classical republics he so much admired. He admired the dignified, independent bearing of its citizens and claimed that in no other country was there such a level of social equality among white men. He also admired the South's gentility and old-world manners, claiming that on a journey of 2,000 miles through the cotton states he had not heard a harsh word or seen a violent action. The 'peculiar gentleness of demeanour and quiet courtesy' of the South he attributed to slavery, which he believed had a restraining influence on the slaveowner because of the great power and responsibility with which he was entrusted. The Southern custom of speaking gently to servants and slaves created 'a softness of manner and tone which, in educated people, being united with dignity, and self-possession, gives me the ideal of a well-bred person'. He admitted, however, that 'Severe measures are sometimes needful in subduing a young negro. What then? Is a colt not to be broken because he is vicious?'[18]

Mitchel argued that the industrial North, in its materialism and hypocrisy, was indistinguishable from Britain: 'That Northern sentiment which pretends to be scandalised at the South is British sentiment.' He believed that its attempt to impose its will on the South was essentially the same as Britain's oppression of Ireland, and that in supporting the South 'he was thinking of Ireland, and contending for the South as the Ireland of this continent'.[19] The interests of North and South were

> substantially the same as the opposing interests of England and Ireland. The one is the commercial, manufacturing, and money-broking power – the other represents mainly agriculture. England has striven long and hard to make the industry of Ireland subservient to herself – that she may have the use of Irish produce . . . Differential duties compel us to take Massachusetts manufactures, and there is even a great and increasing *absentee drain* from the South to the North. Northern 'literature', being cheap and vile, is forced into all our houses; and men of enterprise and of genius at the South go to the North for their career and their reward. You perceive that I am narrating, in part, the history of Ireland.
>
> . . . The actual descent and affinity of the Southern population is in far the greater part Irish, French, Welsh, Spanish – in any case Celtic . . . The Celtic is the superior breed; of finer origin, more fiery brain, more passionate heart – less greedy, grabbing, griping and grovelling . . .
>
> In race being Celtic; in pursuits agricultural; in temperament pleasure loving, hospitable and indolent; in position defensive against the commercial spirit of the age – the South is a new Ireland; her rival another England. Can you wonder that I am a Southerner?[20]

But he also found significant differences between the South and Ireland: Southerners held arms, and did not have a powerful foreign garrison in their midst. 'In short they are strong, free, proud and masters of the situation. The remedy here as in Ireland is repeal of the union. Singular, that your correspondent, in whatever hemisphere he may be, finds himself labouring at repealing of unions. There is nothing like consistency.'[21] This was his standard answer to those who accused him of hypocrisy in advocating freedom for Ireland and slavery in America: 'The liberty which I sought for Ireland was national independence only; and that only was what I sought for the South.'[22]

The *Southern Citizen* sold reasonably well, but Mitchel and Swan believed that its influence was limited because it was published in Knoxville, and decided to transfer it to Washington. In December 1858 Mitchel and his family moved to Washington and took a house on Capitol Hill. Mitchel did not much like Washington, with its vast corps of political lobbyists and intriguers, but he enjoyed mingling with Southern senators and congressmen (almost never with Northerners). His championing of the South did not prevent him from keeping a close eye on European affairs, and in the summer of 1859 he detected the possibility of a breach between France and England. As Anglo–French relations worsened, Mitchel believed that war between the old enemies was imminent, and he grew restless in Washington and decided he could best serve Irish interests by moving to Paris. In July 1859 he and Swan decided to wind up the *Southern Citizen*, and in August 1859 Mitchel sailed from New York for Le Havre.

Travelling to Paris through northern France, Mitchel compared his journey to that of Wolfe Tone over sixty years before, but unlike Tone he had little success in persuading the French government to take an interest in Ireland. After a few weeks in Paris he recognised that neither country was really intent on war, and that he would have been as well remaining at home. He stayed at a small hotel in the Faubourg St Honoré, and in October was visited by John Martin, his brother William and his sisters Margaret and Matilda.

Mitchel also paid several visits to Colonel Miles Byrne, a United Irish veteran who had left Ireland after the 1803 rising and had a long and distinguished career in the French army. He greatly admired and respected Byrne, now eighty years old, and the two became good friends, although Mitchel noted that he was now 'very frail and tells one the same old story too often'.[23] He had few other friends in Paris and was mostly lonely and depressed; his health also suffered in the damp Paris winter. Eventually the loneliness of life in Paris got to him and he concluded: 'Lurking in Paris, waiting for wars, and looking out for squalls, won't do' and decided to return home to Washington in February 1860.[24] But he had only been back a few months when his natural restlessness reasserted itself and he made a snap decision to return to Paris, taking his family with him. He hoped to work as a correspondent for some American and Irish newspapers, and Jenny believed that Paris would be a good place to educate her daughters. In September the Mitchels travelled to Paris, and rented an apartment in the Rue de l'Est, overlooking the Luxembourg Gardens, until May 1861 (and afterwards a cottage in Choisy-le-Roi, in the suburbs). Mitchel supported himself by working as a correspondent for the *Charleston Standard*, the *Irish American* and the *Irishman*, generally living a quiet life, and went on walking tours with his brother William to Normandy (March 1862) and to the south with Martin that summer. He corresponded regularly with his Irish friends about Irish affairs and reiterated his opinion that little would come of such peaceful agitations as the great national petition for a plebiscite on Irish self-government which then preoccupied Irish nationalists. He despaired of the lethargy of Irish politics and claimed that the Irish were 'a scandal to mankind and the shame of the Caucasian race'.[25] He believed that his conviction for treason-felony by a packed jury had shown the hypocrisy and bankruptcy of British government in Ireland, but still his countrymen looked to that same government for concessions and favours. In May 1861, however, probably at Martin's prompting, he agreed to meet The O'Donoghue at Boulogne. Although MP for County Tipperary, O'Donoghue was a fervent advocate of Irish abstention from parliament. He outlined to Mitchel his plan to create a legal, broadly based nationalist organisation which would harness the efforts of all nationalists, including Fenians, and would also utilise the weapon of withdrawal from Westminster. Mitchel was impressed by O'Donoghue and approved of his scheme, and wrote to John O'Mahony recommending that the Fenians support him. In the event, O'Donoghue's plan was stalled by the opposition of Dublin Fenians and the suspicions of conservative constitutional nationalists.[26]

Mitchel also kept closely in touch with events in America, approving strongly of the secession of several southern states in February 1861. When war finally broke out in May, the Mitchels anxiously awaited news from their two eldest boys, John and James, who had remained behind in America and joined the Confederate army. John held a commission in the First South Carolina Artillery, commanding a battery that had shelled Fort Sumter in the action that had started the war. James enlisted as a private in the First Virginia Infantry and was later commissioned in the same regiment; he fought at the first battle of Bull Run (Manassas) on 21 July 1861, in which the Confederates had successfully repulsed a Federal army advance, but it was several months later that his parents received a letter from him and learned that he was safe.[27]

By the autumn of 1862 Mitchel was considering returning to America to be closer to his sons. He had little enough to do in Paris: his reports for the *Charleston Mercury* were stopped by the Union naval blockade of the Confederacy, and he had ceased to write for the *Irishman*. Moreover, his youngest son William, now eighteen, was anxious to join his brothers in fighting for the Confederacy.

Father and son sailed for New York in September 1862 and on to Baltimore, where they made contact with a Confederate committee that helped people cross the Potomac into the Confederacy. Waiting to cross the river with eleven others, Mitchel stayed at house of a Southern sympathiser, but was betrayed by an Irishman who recognised him. The house was raided, but Mitchel, suspicious of the Irishman, had already left and hidden in the nearby woods. In the end he and a few others bought a leaky skiff from a local fisherman and, running the gauntlet of Union patrol boats, crossed the Potomac at night and entered Confederate territory on 24 October 1862. The Mitchels travelled on to Richmond, Virginia, capital of the Confederacy, and William immediately enlisted as a private in the First Virginia Infantry, his brother James's regiment. Mitchel also tried to enlist but was disqualified because of his short-sightedness. He did, however, serve with an ambulance committee which, as well as tending to the wounded, occasionally did guard duty in the trenches around Richmond. Mitchel also put his pen at the service of the Confederacy, accepting the editorship of the *Richmond Enquirer*, a semi-official Confederate newspaper.

Richmond was the main military objective of the Union forces and was defended by the South's best troops, General Robert E. Lee's army of Northern Virginia. Numerous pitched battles and skirmishes were fought in its vicinity, and the city was often in state of near siege. In the summer of 1863 Lee attempted to take the war to the North, but was checked in fierce fighting at Gettysburg (1–3 July). The First Virginia Infantry were in the thick of the fighting: James emerged unscathed, but for several weeks there was no news of William, except that his regiment had been almost annihilated in the great Confederate infantry charge on Cemetery Ridge. Finally on 30 August it was confirmed that William was indeed among the dead. It was news that Mitchel had expected. He learned from a survivor of the battle that Willie had fought with distinction, seizing the regimental colours from a fallen comrade and despite being wounded himself carrying them forward at the head of the regiment until he was finally shot down. Mitchel noted that his son 'could have had no more enviable fate. He died in honourable company'.[28] In Ireland, Jenny Mitchel, on hearing of William's death, resolved to return to America to see her other sons before they too might be killed. Taking her two girls with her (Henrietta had died aged 21 in Paris earlier that year), and without notifying her husband, she ran the Northern blockade and arrived in Richmond towards the end of 1863.

After Gettysburg the war turned against the Confederacy, and Mitchel grew increasingly disillusioned with the Confederate president, Jefferson Davis. In December 1863 he resigned from the *Enquirer* and became the leader-writer for the anti-Davis *Richmond Examiner*. Mitchel was aware that the North, with its vast resources, was growing stronger every day, while the South was growing weaker. He observed that ordinary Southerners, increasingly giving vent to their resentment at a 'rich man's war and a poor man's fight', were not prepared to endure their hardships indefinitely. Mitchel tried to keep up the fighting spirit of the South by pointing out what life would be like in a conquered country, warning of 'disarmings and disenfranchisements and civil disabilities, such as we have experienced in Ireland'.[29]

Mitchel also did his best to rally support for the Confederacy abroad, giving letters of introduction to Confederate agents, Captain Lalor and Father John Bannon, who travelled to Ireland to attempt to discourage Irish enlistment into the Union army.[30] In a letter to the *Nation* Mitchel applauded the bravery of the thousands of Irishmen fighting for the North, but claimed they were dupes, fooled by false promises of land in the South and fighting for a government that despised them: 'They are to be made use of precisely as the poor negroes are – thrust to the front in every fight, and thrown aside afterwards as broken tools. They will never hold land in the Confederate country, save that regular fee-simple of six feet by two which many thousands of them now peacefully hold.'[31]

In 1864 General Ulysses S. Grant, the Union general-in-chief, stepped up his campaign against the Confederacy, and that May saw some particularly savage fighting. Mitchel's ambulance committee was in action at several engagements, notably the bloody and indecisive battle of the Wilderness (5–7 May 1864) and at Spotsylvania (8–19 May), when there seemed to be no end to the dead and wounded carried from the field. Mitchel described the scene as one of 'horror and anguish and filth'; fragments of limbs littered the camp and 'pitiable and horrible cases of ghastly wounds are so frequent on these occasions that one might grow callous to the sight of human agony'. Many Richmond families lost loved ones, but Mitchel observed: 'No sadness shows itself; above all, no cowardice . . . I confess that I delight in the spectacle of a people roused in this way to a full display of all its manhood . . . planting itself firmly on its sown ground, stripped for battle and defying fate.'[32]

Grant continued to press against Richmond, and by June 1864 the city was under siege. In July 1864 Mitchel learned that his eldest son John, commanding the besieged Fort Sumter, had been killed by an artillery shell. James was now the only one of Mitchel's sons who remained alive, and even he had lost an arm at Chancellorsville. But such was the Confederate need for experienced officers that he was back at his post weeks later. Possibly to spare the Mitchel family further grief, James was removed to a staff post in Richmond in September 1864.[33]

In early April 1865 Union forces broke though Lee's lines, and Richmond was evacuated. Mitchel accompanied the Confederate government to Danville, on the southern frontier of Virginia, refusing to concede that the Southern cause was lost. Even after

Lee's surrender to Grant on 9 April, Mitchel remained at large for
some weeks, staying on a friend's farm in Halifax County. On
hearing of the assassination of Abraham Lincoln on 14 April he
observed that 'The malignant and vindictive Yankee mind will take
it as the very luckiest of possible events . . . As for poor Lincoln, he
was an ignoramus and a boor; not an apostle at all; no grand
reformer; not so much as an abolitionist, except by accident – a
man of very small account in every way.'[34] When eventually he
heard of the surrender of the last sizeable body of Confederate
troops, Mitchel returned to Richmond in May. Since there was no
way for him to earn a living there, he resolved to go to New York,
where there were many pro-Southern 'Copperhead' Democrats
and 'plenty of good Irishmen above all, who though they fought
us hard, yet never hated us with the holy hatred of the Puritans'.
Here he accepted the editorship of the *New York Daily News*, a
Democratic newspaper that had opposed the war.[35]

Many Republicans were angered by the presence of this
outspoken champion of the South in New York and called for his
arrest, claiming he was instrumental in the mistreatment of cap-
tured Union soldiers, and some even implied that he had been
involved in the conspiracy to assassinate Lincoln.[36] Mitchel dismissed all such claims out of hand, but refused to condemn
explicitly the assassination of Lincoln. Instead he denounced the
triumphalist and vindictive actions of the Federal government,
particularly Jefferson Davis's imprisonment. He claimed that Davis
had fought an honourable war, and that his imprisonment in harsh
conditions was one of the 'blackest villainies known to history'.[37]
Mitchel claimed that the North was still behaving as a country at
war and was imposing 'every most ingenious and intolerable humiliation' on the South. Warnings to tone down his articles only
spurred him to denounce Yankee triumphalism more vehemently.
Finally, he was arrested at the *Daily News* office on 14 June on a

charge of writing articles critical of the government. He was taken by steamer to Fortress Monroe, Virginia, where Jefferson Davis and Senator Clement Claiborne Clay (accused of conspiracy to assassinate Lincoln) were the only other prisoners, arriving there on 17 June.[38]

The prison regime was extremely harsh: his cell was small and damp, the food almost inedible and served without plates or cutlery, and he was allowed no exercise, writing materials or tobacco. He had difficulty sleeping, kept awake by the scurrying of rats and the buzzing of mosquitoes, and he suffered severe asthma attacks. While in prison he learned that his mother had died in Ireland some months earlier – the Union blockade had prevented word from reaching him in Richmond – news that was a further blow to him. On 10 August he was examined by a prison doctor who informed the authorities that would die unless he was better fed and allowed exercise. Thereafter his conditions improved: he was given books, newspapers and better food, and allowed to walk in the open air. His health improved but never really recovered from the damage done in the first two months. He aged significantly during this period, becoming a little stooped and looking haggard and worn beyond his fifty years.[39]

Many Irish-Americans who had supported the North, such as John O'Mahony and Richard O'Gorman, complained to the authorities about his treatment. The Fenian movement, which had grown rapidly in the Union army during the war, made strong representations on Mitchel's behalf to the Federal government, and he was released on 30 October 1865. Mitchel considered taking legal action to challenge his arrest, but his lawyers advised that he would probably be arrested again if he made any trouble and it would be better for him to go to Europe until passions cooled in America.[40] Reflecting on his arrest, he concluded:

I suppose that I am the only person who has ever been a prisoner of state to the British and American government one after the other. It is true, the English government took care to have a special act of parliament passed for my incarceration: but our Yankees disdain in these days to make any pretence of law at all . . . And these two governments, we are told, are the very highest expression and grandest hope of the civilisation of the nineteenth century. Here is the very point, I suspect. I despise the civilisation of the nineteenth century, and its two highest expressions and grandest hopes, most especially – so the said century sees nothing that can be done with me, except to tie me up . . . They are both in the wrong: but then, if I am able to put them in the wrong, they are able to put me into dungeons.[41]

CHAPTER 7

Fenians and Home Rule, 1865-75

After his release Mitchel was offered the position of Fenian financial agent in Paris, with a generous salary of $2,500 a year. He had always had reservations about Fenianism, as he had about all secret conspiracies, trusting instead in the Carlylean notion of spontaneous revolution, but he accepted the position because he believed that the movement might now actually achieve something. Relations between Britain and America were strained after the civil war, and the Fenians, who included thousands of battle-hardened soldiers, appeared to be a much more formidable organisation. On 10 November Mitchel sailed for France. Alone in Paris, he brooded on the events of the past years. The war had taken a heavy toll on him and his family. He observed that they had suffered heavily for their support of the Confederacy, 'and although it was a good cause, I must admit that I grudge it what it has cost us – the lives of two sons in defence of a country, which after all, was not their own'.[1]

He carried out his business for the Fenians dutifully in Paris from lodgings in Rue Richer and later at his old quarters in the Rue Lacépède. As well as dispensing Fenian money, he had been entrusted with gaining French government support for Irish nationalism, but soon realised that this was useless. He remained unimpressed by the Fenian leadership, especially James Stephens, whom he believed had shown a lack of courage when conditions were at their most favourable for insurrection in the early months of 1866. He also disliked Stephens personally, a feeling that was mutual: Stephens regarded Mitchel as 'a disgruntled egoist and a man of the past'. Moreover, Stephens's optimistic accounts of the strength of Fenianism in Ireland did not tally with the information Mitchel was receiving from Kenyon and Martin. Far from mounting a major rising soon, it seemed that the Fenian movement in Ireland was settling back into its usual cloak-and-dagger ineffectiveness. Mitchel also became increasingly frustrated with American Fenianism, as it splintered into different factions, one intent on attacking Britain through Canada, another concentrating on insurrection in Ireland. Disillusioned, he resigned his position on 22 June 1866, writing to Stephens that, as he had lost all hope of communicating with the French government, he did not think it right to draw a large salary merely to receive and pay over sums of money, something that could easily be done without him.[2]

After his resignation Mitchel supported himself by writing for the *New York Daily News*, but mostly he was lonely and missed his family. In October 1866 he returned to Richmond, where he lived for the next year, writing his *History of Ireland from the Treaty of Limerick* (1867). This was mainly a denunciation of centuries of British oppression in Ireland, reprising large chunks of works such as his own *Last Conquest* and Wolfe Tone's journals. Mitchel himself was dissatisfied with the completed work, but it had many admirers and became a standard nationalist history.

In October 1867 he moved to New York and founded another newspaper, the *Irish Citizen*, which was strongly critical of the Fenian movement. In February 1867 an attempt had been made to unite Fenianism under Mitchel's leadership, but he had declined. He had no wish 'to take and knit up the two ragged fag ends of an organisation originally rotten and now all tattered and torn, and to wear the patched up thing as a robe of honour'; he refused to commission generals for a phantom army or engage in the fiction that an Irish republic had already been established. Although he praised the courage of the Fenians who had fought in the insurrection of March 1867, he deplored that they had not been better led or more usefully deployed. He stressed that his opposition to Fenianism did not mean that he opposed Fenian methods: 'The Irish have the clear right to strike at England anywhere or anyhow, in Canada, in Ireland, in London, by steel or gunpowder or firewood. But I hold that those who undertake such warfare at present, whether civilised or uncivilised, must perish and perish in vain.'[3]

Mitchel claimed that he was entitled to call himself 'the father of Fenianism': twenty years earlier he had proclaimed Fenian principles 'to their most revolutionary extent, and had suffered for it'; but he stressed that he was father of 'the principle of Fenianism, not of its existing forms and organisation'. In a series of letters to John Martin in the *Irish Citizen* Mitchel outlined his main criticisms of Fenianism. It was 'established upon a wrong and false basis by that wretched Stephens', who had deluded everyone about the movement's strength. Furthermore, Mitchel regarded membership of a secret oath-bound organisation as inconsistent with the duties of an American citizen. Fenianism's plan to mount an immediate insurrection against England, using Irish-American men and arms, was fatally flawed: while England and America were at peace such efforts would contravene American law and would never be allowed by the American government. Just as the Southern states had lost when they had taken on a more powerful and populous enemy, so Ireland could never beat England unless she was engaged in a general European war or, better still, a war with America. Until this happened there was no point in collecting money that would surely be squandered in secret conspiracy. Instead Irishmen should join their local militias and wait for their opportunity. And if in the meantime that 'enormous sack of gas' called Fenianism should collapse beneath the weight of its factions, pretensions and delusions, then Ireland would be none the worse.[4]

In private letters Mitchel was even more scathing about American Fenianism, claiming that it was a fraud that actually inhibited Irish-American efforts for Irish independence: 'Very many gallant and worthy fellows (but terribly ignorant) have been in the movement – but the best of them . . . are dead or picking oakum.' He believed that it would be better for a new organisation to replace the Fenians, and he endorsed the founding of the Irish Confederation in March 1872. This body was established to unite all Irish-American political organisations but had little success and most American Fenians did not join.[5]

Mitchel also reserved his quota of scorn for constitutional nationalists, in particular the Home Rule movement launched by Isaac Butt in May 1870. He wrote to Martin that he had 'never esteemed Butt, neither in an intellectual nor in a moral nor in a patriotic sense. He is a humbug.' He was contemptuous of the movement's reliance on constitutional methods and its aspirations to limited self-government. Under the current restricted franchise, he regarded the Irish electorate as the equivalent of a packed jury, designed to return members to do the bidding of the British government.[6] Mitchel's opposition to Home Rule was not softened even when Martin (now Mitchel's brother-in-law, having married his youngest sister Henrietta (1827–1913) in 1868 after a twenty-year courtship) became the Home Government Association's first MP, winning a by-election in Meath in January 1871, and later became secretary of the Home Rule League.

The *Irish Citizen* also condemned the apparently conciliatory Irish policy of Liberals such as Gladstone and Bright as another instalment of British hypocrisy, claiming that their intention was simply to 'more rapidly and completely extirpate' the Irish people. Mitchel dismissed the disestablishment of the Church of Ireland under legislation enacted in July 1869 as a fraud: he maintained that the British government were simply appropriating church revenues for their own use and that the burden on the Irish peasantry would in no way be eased.[7]

On European affairs he was highly critical of the manner of Italian and German unification, claiming that the right of a nation to unify itself had become the latest excuse for tyranny, with powerful states simply swallowing up their weaker neighbours: 'So Italy unified herself under the inspiration of Cavour; and Bismarck is only imitating that brigand Piedmontese.'[8] Mitchel's opposition to centralisation also led him to sympathise with the Paris communards of 1871. He claimed that they were not communists or atheists, but republicans who had fought gallantly for local autonomy, and that they were the victims rather than the perpetrators of atrocities. He was adamant that they should not be confused with the International Working Men's Association, founded to establish international co-operation among socialist, communist and revolutionary groups, which he regarded as 'a most senseless and noxious sort of association'. On hearing that the International had established a branch in Cork, Mitchel was dismissive, noting that 'They are not theorists, our good Irish, and do not believe in Karl Marx.' He maintained that 'this International solidarity, as they call it, is violently anti-national' and would do nothing to improve the life of the working man. He predicted that 'A great battle will yet be fought, between common property on one side and common sense on the other.'[9]

On domestic affairs, the *Irish Citizen* was strongly Democratic and sharply criticised the vindictiveness of Radical Republicans towards the South, where it claimed that whites were being discriminated against in favour of blacks. Mitchel dismissed accounts of Ku Klux Klan violence against blacks as fabrications and denounced emancipation as a 'monstrous crime', typical of the short-sighted philanthropy of the age, that had set the slaves free without any means of providing for themselves; he claimed that most longed for the return of slavery and the protection of their masters.[10]

Such views led John Blake Dillon to accuse him of allowing his antipathy to the Yankees to blind him to the future of humanity. Mitchel retorted:

> Poor humanity! If it depends for its future upon the Yankees it is going to have a damned bad time. Yes, I believe in the future of humanity and that its future will be very much like its past: that is, pretty mean . . . Future of humanity be damned – why, I don't believe in the present, let alone the future.[11]

Mitchel's harsh view of the world pointedly repudiated the Enlightenment tradition of humane liberalism. On one occasion he refused to visit a lunatic asylum in Jackson, Mississippi, on the grounds that 'I bitterly hate lunatics and cannot bear the glare of a mad eye'; he also believed that epidemics were useful in disposing of the sickly 'who would otherwise linger and even propagate perhaps their unhappy species'.[12]

Many contemporaries spoke of Mitchel as a man who appeared to belong to a different age: his admirers often compared his stern stoicism to that of the ancient Greeks and Romans. Certainly he bore his misfortunes with great fortitude and was dismissive of the modern preoccupation with happiness: 'We are not in this world for the purpose of getting ourselves made "happy", but for the purpose of doing and suffering what it is our duty to do and suffer.'[13] In political terms, his pessimistic rejection of progress, his suspicion of centralised power and his refusal to grant the benefits of citizenship to criminals, slaves or corrupt aristocrats owed more to an austere classical republicanism than to any contemporary ideology.[14]

Mitchel continued to be active in Irish-American affairs and in January 1871 was one of the committee that welcomed the 'Cuba Five', amnestied Fenian prisoners who included John Devoy and Jeremiah O'Donovan Rossa. He edited the *Irish Citizen* until July 1872, but by this stage his health was failing, and he had to bring the paper to an end.

During the winter of 1872–3 Mitchel, as an elder statesman of Irish nationalism, was asked by the *Irish American* newspaper to respond to the anti-Irish lectures given in America by the English historian James Anthony Froude, based on the first volume of his controversial work *The English in Ireland in the Eighteenth Century* (1872). In a series of public lectures and published letters Mitchel attacked Froude for his sectarian bias and for falsifying Irish history, in particular his reliance on the lurid and unreliable depositions relating to the rising of 1641 which grossly exaggerated the scale of the massacre of Protestants. The letters were afterwards published in book form as *The Crusade of the Period* (1873), but they were the work of a tired crusader and lack the savage indignation and memorably cutting phrases of his earlier work. He also gave a series of lectures in 1874 on behalf of Clan na Gael and donated his fees for the rescue of Fenian prisoners from Australia.[15]

In the summer of 1873 Mitchel had to cope with more family tragedy. James Mitchel's wife and young daughter, who had been a great favourite of Mitchel's, died within a week of each other. Mitchel keenly felt his son's grief. (James later remarried, and his son John Purroy Mitchel (1879–1918) became mayor of New York City in 1913.) By now Mitchel's health was so poor and his energy and strength had so deserted him that he found it difficult to write or lecture, and he fell into poverty. His situation came to the attention of John and William Dillon, sons of his old friend John Blake Dillon, who raised a testimonial of £2,000 for him in November 1873. Mitchel was somewhat embarrassed by this, but he grew closer to the young Dillons and more drawn into Irish politics, and in the general election of February 1874 he allowed himself to be put forward as an independent nationalist candidate for Cork city. He had no intention of taking his seat if elected, but he knew that as an unpardoned rebel his candidature would arouse controversy and remind the Irish people that there was an alternative to the peaceful pursuit of Home Rule. In the event, his bitter opposition to Home Rule had little appeal for the voters of Cork, and the two seats were won by Home Rule candidates, with Mitchel finishing bottom of the poll. Undeterred, in June 1874 he wrote to John Dillon that he might return to Ireland to stand for parliament in person.[16] The following month he decided to go to Ireland, accompanied by his daughter Isabel. It was 26 years since he had been transported from Ireland, and he was powerfully moved by his first sight of the Irish coast.

He arrived in Queenstown at the end of July, and stayed a few days in Cork, before travelling north to see his sisters in County Down. In September he went to Dublin but was so 'savage against that help- less, driftless concern called "Home Rule"' that he refused to stay under the roof of any Home Ruler in Dublin – even John Martin – and he took lodgings at 31 Holles Street. He was much visited and received many invitations, most of which he refused, but he and Isabel did attend a dinner at Lady Wilde's house in Merrion Square, at which the famous patriot and his beautiful daughter were much admired. His return confronted the authorities with a dilemma. They maintained that he had broken his parole and was liable to arrest, but since the original term of his sentence had elapsed and transportation was now abolished, they realised that arresting him risked stirring up a hornet's nest of legal and political difficulties, and settled instead for keeping a close watch on his movements.[17]

Mitchel returned to New York in October. While in Ireland he had agreed that he would stand for parliament if a vacancy occurred.

In February 1875 he learned there was to be a by-election in County Tipperary and, despite his worsening health, he returned to Ireland, this time with his son James. In a statement written before his arrival he maintained that his attitude to parliamentary politics had not changed: his intention was to 'spit upon the franchise which they pretend to allow us and especially to overthrow the whole system of parliamentary representation . . . the most delusive machinery by which our oppression is carried on'.[18] With such an outspoken opponent of Home Rule offering himself for election, the Home Rule Party was in an awkward position. A statement from John Martin published in the nationalist press skirted around their differences: he acknowledged Mitchel's opposition to Home Rule but claimed that should he be elected 'the national dignity of our country will not suffer in his hands'.[19]

Mindful of his earlier experience in Cork, Mitchel tempered his opposition to Home Rule in his election address, declaring that he was in favour of 'Home Rule' as he understood it, 'that is, the sovereign independence of Ireland'. He also stood on a platform of tenant right, an end to evictions, free education, and an amnesty for Fenian prisoners, but in reality he was standing as the embodiment of militant nationalism: a man who had never deviated from his opposition to British rule and had suffered for his convictions. He landed at Queenstown on 17 February to find that he had already been elected. The nomination had taken place the previous day, and as Mitchel was the only candidate nominated, he was declared elected. Some days later parliament declared him ineligible as an undischarged felon, but Mitchel decided to stand for the seat again, announcing that he would do so as often as he was unseated. His candidature was endorsed by Charles Stewart Parnell, who had recently joined the Home Rule Party and who contributed £25 to his election expenses. Mitchel addressed a large crowd in Tipperary town on 18 February, and attempted to do the same that night in Clonmel, but he was now so weak that he could only say a few words. The young William O'Brien, who had been active in his election campaign, noticed how he constantly gasped for breath and thought that only his 'indomitable will' was keeping him alive.[20]

After a couple of weeks attempting to recuperate in Cork, Mitchel travelled to Dublin on 9 March and then on to his child-hood home of Dromalane, near Newry, on 11 March. Another poll took place in Tipperary on 11 March, and this time a Tory candi-date contested the seat: Mitchel beat him by 3,114 votes to 746. Rejoicing in his victory, he maintained that 'The chief fact about my past life which recommended me to the people of Tipperary was that I had made no peace with England.'[21]

Over the next few days his health declined rapidly, and he died at Dromalane on the morning of 20 March 1875. He was buried in his parents' grave in the Unitarian cemetery, High Street, Newry, where a monument erected by his widow marks his grave. Over 10,000 people attended his funeral. Among them was John Martin, already seriously ill, who died a week later.

Conclusion

For most of his lifetime Mitchel's influence on events in Ireland was muted. He was contemptuous of the compromises and piecemeal gains of practical politics, and spelled out little in the way of a political programme. He was not a systematic thinker: his political philosophy mirrored his temperament, veering between austere stoicism and romantic excess. Moreover, he was a difficult man to work with, usually at odds with his fellow nationalists: his tendency to regard himself as the lone champion of rectitude, clear thinking and plain speaking left little room for co-operation with those who disagreed with him in any way. He recognised this himself, joking that 'I have long felt myself to be a party of one member – a party whose basis of action is to think and act for itself, whose one fundamental rule is to speak its mind . . . and in its proceedings I assure you there reigns the most unbroken unanimity.'[1] This incapacity to work with others often condemned him to political ineffectiveness: the very vehemence of his language – the railing, the repetition, the violently provocative rhetoric – often seems born out of frustration at his own political impotence.

In the longer term, however, Mitchel proved to be a highly influential figure. His contention that the Famine was deliberate genocide became widely accepted, and greatly reinforced the bitterness and resentment of many Irish nationalists towards England. Mitchel was the key nineteenth-century figure in the revival of

militant republicanism: his calls in the *United Irishman* to emulate
the republican revolutionaries of 1798 were phrased in language of
a kind that had not been openly aired in Ireland for half a century.
His writings would inspire a wide range of nationalists including
Douglas Hyde, John Devoy, Eoin MacNeill, Constance Markievicz,
Arthur Griffith, James Connolly and Patrick Pearse.[2] Pearse saw
him as a key figure in apostolic succession of nationalist heroes
from Wolfe Tone and regarded the *Jail Journal* as 'the last gospel of
the New Testament of Irish nationality'. He thrilled to Mitchel's
advocacy of the power of bloodshed to redeem the soul of an abject
nation, seeing him as a prophet who delivered 'God's word to man,
delivered it fiery-tongued'. He lauded Mitchel's hatred of 'the
English empire, of English commercialism supported by English
militarism, a thing wholly evil, perhaps the most evil thing there
has ever been in the world', and maintained that 'such hate is not
only a good thing, but it is a duty'.[3]

Mitchel's emphasis on national and individual self-reliance was a
particularly strong influence on Arthur Griffith, who described him
as a 'proud, fiery-hearted, electric-brained, giant-souled Irishman
who stood up to the might of the whole British empire'; Griffith
maintained that he was 'the greatest figure we have amongst us'.
He argued that Mitchel's militant agrarian policy was the inspiration behind the Land League, and also took him as a guide for
contemporary politics, seeing only treachery in any alliance with
British Liberals. While most other nationalists ignored Mitchel's
racist and inhumane pronouncements, Griffith endorsed them.
In language that could have been transcribed from Mitchel he
denounced the 'flabby doctrine that has gained some vogue in
Ireland – mortally afraid of being esteemed behind "The Age",
or limping in the rear of "Progressive Thought" – that an Irish
Nationalist must by very virtue of being a nationalist subscribe to
and swallow all the Isms of Sentimentalism'. Griffith believed that

Mitchel had performed 'essential work' in 'dissevering the case for Irish independence from theories of humanitarianism and universalism'. The early Sinn Féin adopted many of Mitchel's ideas, strongly proclaiming its opposition to contemporary liberalism and denouncing free trade as the battering-ram of British imperialism.[4]

Despite his contempt for constitutional politics, Mitchel also had a strong influence on some of the more trenchant members of the Irish Parliamentary Party. Leading members such as John Dillon, Michael Davitt, William Redmond and Tim Healy all fell under his spell in one way or another (although despite his admiration for Mitchel's lifelong resistance to British imperialism, Davitt was appalled by his inhumanity towards convicts).[5] Nobody denounced British rule as fiercely as Mitchel, and while Ireland remained under British rule his fierce anglophobe rhetoric struck a chord with many Irish nationalists.

In vehemently rejecting the prevailing nineteenth-century values of progress and liberalism, Mitchel placed himself on the margins of political life for much of that century, but he also positioned himself to be an important influence in shaping a twentieth-century Irish nationalism that rejected many liberal values and assumptions. After the onset of the great depression in 1873, orthodox nineteenth-century liberalism had a growing number of critics and Mitchel's ferocious anti-liberalism found a more receptive audience. Early twentieth-century Irish nationalism was often characterised by an introspective and backward-looking romanticism that saw little of value in contemporary industrial society and despised the modern preoccupation with material comfort and prosperity. It did not balk at bloodshed – indeed, it welcomed it – if this was the price to be paid to awaken modern society from its complacency and materialism. Aodh de Blácam wrote that in Mitchel's denunciation of nineteenth-century liberalism 'it is not one man, but Irish nationhood itself, with its wrathful rejection of materialism, that we hear'.[6]

Mitchel's influence was strongest on the generation that brought about Irish independence: between 1917 and 1938, four biographies of him were published, all favourable. But after 1938 little enough was written on him, and from the 1970s he became a *bête noire* for many historians. Once Irish independence had actually been achieved and consolidated, his fierce denunciations of British rule seemed excessive and even disturbing, and his writings provide ample material for those who wish to highlight the dark side of Irish nationalism. Views that shocked contemporaries by their harshness and inhumanity are even more likely to shock today, given our greater awareness of the destructive consequences of racial prejudice and nationalist hatred. Clearly there is much in Mitchel's thinking that now seems outmoded and even repugnant, but such feelings should not blind us to the extent of his influence. Mitchel is an easy figure to deplore, but one who cannot be ignored. His fierce and uncompromising rhetoric wove its way into the fabric of Irish nationalism and formed one of its most influential and resilient strands.

Notes

Introduction

1 W. B. Yeats, *Autobiographies* (London, 1966), p. 225; Tom Garvin, 'O'Connell and the making of Irish political culture' in M. R. O'Connell (ed.), *Daniel O'Connell: Political Pioneer* (Dublin, 1991), p. 11; R. F. Foster, *Modern Ireland 1600–1972* (London, 1982), p. 316; R. V. Comerford, *The Fenians in Context: Irish Politics and Society 1848–82* (Dublin, 1985), p. 37; Malcolm Brown, *The Politics of Irish Literature: From Thomas Davis to W. B. Yeats* (London, 1972), p. 138.

Chapter 1: *Youth and Early Life, 1815–45*

1 William Dillon, *Life of John Mitchel* (2 vols, London, 1888), I, p. 8; J. A. Froude, *Thomas Carlyle* (2 vols, London, 1884), I, p. 399.

2 John Bannon, *The Life of John Mitchel* (Liverpool, 1882), pp. 13–15.

3 Mitchel to John Mitchel senior, 17 July 1834 (PRONI, D/1078/M/2); Bannon, *Mitchel*, pp. 18–19.

4 Dillon, *Mitchel*, I, pp. 26–9; II, p. 268; Michael Cavanagh, 'Biography of John Mitchel' (NLI, MS 3225).

5 Dillon, *Mitchel*, I, p. 41.

6 Mitchel to Martin, 29 Nov. 1838 (Dillon, *Mitchel*, I, p. 37).

7 Dillon, *Mitchel*, I, pp. 93, 167; description of Martin by John Augustus O'Shea (Belfast Central Library, F. J. Bigger collection (hereafter Bigger coll.), Z314(1)).

8 C. G. Duffy, *Young Ireland: A Fragment of Irish History* (London, 1880), pp. 730–1; idem, *My Life in Two Hemispheres* (2 vols, London, 1903), I, p. 62.

9 John Mitchel, *The Last Conquest of Ireland (Perhaps)* (Glasgow, 1861), p. 82; *Nation*, 13, 27 May 1843; Dillon, *Mitchel*, I, p. 71.

10 Duffy, *Young Ireland*, p. 302.

11 Mitchel to Martin, 21 June 1844 (Dillon, *Mitchel*, I, pp. 53–4).

Chapter 2: *The Nation, 1845–7*

1   *Nation*, 22 Nov. 1845.

2   C. G. Duffy, *Four Years of Irish History, 1845–9* (London, 1883), pp. 117–18.

3   *Nation*, 28 Feb., 7 Mar., 4 Apr. 1846.

4   C. G. Duffy, *My Life in Two Hemispheres* (2 vols, London, 1903), I, pp. 135–6, 138.

5   John Mitchel, *The Last Conquest of Ireland (Perhaps)* (Glasgow, 1861), p. 114.

6   Mitchel to Martin, *c.* May 1846 (William Dillon, *Life of John Mitchel* (2 vols, London, 1888), I, p. 111); *Nation*, 10 Jan., 21 Mar. 1846.

7   Mitchel to Duffy, 22 Aug., 11 Sept. 1845 (NLI, MS 5756/183, 191).

8   J. A. Froude, *Thomas Carlyle* (2 vols, London, 1884), I, p. 399; C. G. Duffy, *Conversations with Carlyle* (London, 1892), pp. 26–7; see also Carlyle to William Mitchel, 20 Jan. 1852 (Bigger coll., z314(3)).

9   *Nation*, 18 July 1846.

10 Duffy, *Four Years*, p. 237

11 *Nation*, 18, 25 July, 1 Aug. 1846.

12 Mitchel to M. J. Barry, [25] July 1846 (RIA, MS 12/P/16 II no. 15); *Nation*, 30 Dec. 1846; Mitchel to O'Brien, 30 Dec. 1846 (NLI, MS 437/1747).

13 *Nation*, 22 Aug. 1846.

14 Irish Confederation minute books (RIA, MS 23/H/43).

15 J. F. Lalor, 'A new nation', *Nation*, 24 Apr. 1847; idem, 'Tenants' right and landlord law', *Nation*, 15 May 1847.

16 *Irish Felon*, 26 June, 1 July 1848.

17 Mitchel to O'Brien, 24 Apr. 1847 (NLI, MS 438/1882).

18 Lalor to Mitchel, 21 June 1847 (RIA, MS 12/P/15 I(4)).

19 Mitchel to O'Brien, 8 Sept. 1847 (NLI, MS 438/1983).

20 *Nation*, 6, 23 Nov. 1847, 5 Feb. 1848; Dillon, *Mitchel*, I, pp. 173–5.

21 Mitchel, *Last Conquest*, pp. 147–8.

22 *Nation*, 17 Apr., 29 May, 11, 18, 25 Sept. 1847.

23 Mitchel, *Last Conquest*, p. 143.

24 C. E. Trevelyan, *The Irish Crisis* (London, 1848), p. 201. On providentialism see especially Peter Gray, *Famine, Land and Politics: British Government and Irish Society, 1843–50* (Dublin, 1999), pp. 96–106, 256–83, 322–7.

25 Mitchel, *Last Conquest*, p. 219.

26 See, for example, James S. Donnelly, jr, *The Great Irish Potato Famine* (Stroud, 2002), pp. 18–20; Gerry Kearns, '"Educate that holy hatred": place, trauma and identity in the Irish nationalism of John Mitchel', *Political Geography* XX: 7 (Sept. 2001), pp. 885–911.

27   Mitchel to Kenyon, *c*. Nov. 1857 (Dillon, *Mitchel*, II, pp. 104–6); *Nation*, 10, 17 Apr. 1847.

28   John Mitchel, *Jail Journal, or Five Years in British Prisons* (enlarged edn, with a preface by Arthur Griffith, Dublin, [1913]), p. 87; idem, *Last Conquest*, p. 136; *United Irishman*, 4 Mar. 1848.

29   *Nation*, 16 Sept., 2 Oct., 20, 27 Nov. 1847.

30   *Nation*, 8 Jan. 1848.

31   Mitchel to Lalor, 4 Jan. 1848 (L. Fogarty (ed.), *James Fintan Lalor* (Dublin, 1918), pp. 120–3).

32   Mitchel to O'Brien, 19 Mar. 1847 (NLI, MS 438/1845); Mitchel, *Last Conquest*, p. 149.

33   *Nation*, 8, 15 Jan. 1848; Mitchel to Martin, 8 Aug. 1847 (Dillon, *Mitchel*, I, p. 166).

34   O'Brien to Duffy, 29 Dec. [1847] (NLI, MS 2642/3473).

35   *Nation*, 5 Feb. 1848; Robert Sloan, *William Smith O'Brien and the Young Ireland Rebellion of 1848* (Dublin, 2000), p. 206.

36   *Nation*, 5 Feb. 1848.

37   Duffy, *Four Years*, pp. 493–4.

38   For the entire debate see *Nation*, 5 Feb. 1848; Duffy, *Four Years*, p. 491.

Chapter 3: *United Irishman, 1848*

1   John Mitchel, *The Last Conquest of Ireland (Perhaps)* (Glasgow, 1861), p. 159.

2   James Clarence Mangan, *Poems*, ed. D. J. O'Donoghue (Dublin, 1903), p. xxviii; Ellen Shannon Mangan, *James Clarence Mangan* (Dublin, 1996), pp. 165, 315.

3   *United Irishman*, 12 Feb. 1848.

4   Michael Doheny, *The Felon's Track* (Dublin, 1918), p. 127.

5   *United Irishman*, 4 Mar. 1848.

6   *United Irishman*, 12 Feb. 1848.

7   T. D. Reilly, 'The French fashion', *United Irishman*, 4 Mar. 1848.

8   *United Irishman*, 22 Apr., 13 May 1848.

9   *United Irishman*, 4, 25 Mar. 1848.

10   C. G. Duffy, *My Life in Two Hemispheres* (2 vols, London, 1903), I, pp. 261–2.

11   *Freeman's Journal*, 8 Mar. 1848; *Nation*, 8 Apr. 1848; *United Irishman*, 8 Apr. 1848.

12   *United Irishman*, 11, 18 Mar. 1848; John Mitchel, *Jail Journal, or Five Years in British Prisons* (enlarged edn with a preface by Arthur Griffith, Dublin, [1913]), p. 81.

13   *United Irishman*, 18 Mar. 1848.

14   Mitchel, *Jail Journal*, pp. 69–70.

15 *United Irishman*, 15, 29 Apr. 1848.

16 *United Irishman*, 29 Apr. 1848.

17 Mitchel, *Jail Journal*, pp. 147–8, 78–9; on tensions in Mitchel's social thinking see John Newsinger, 'John Mitchel and Irish nationalism', *Literature and History* VI (1980), pp. 182–200.

18 *United Irishman*, 29 Apr. 1848.

19 Mitchel to —— , 10 Apr. 1848 (NLI, MS 33898); Mitchel to —— , 20 June 1858 (William Dillon, *Life of John Mitchel* (2 vols, London, 1888), II, p. 130); Mitchel, *Jail Journal*, p. 81.

20 Mitchel, *Jail Journal*, p. 147.

21 Dillon, *Mitchel*, II, p. 259.

22 Duffy, *My Life*, I, p. 269.

23 O'Brien to Duffy, 24 Mar. 1848 (NLI, MS 2642/3480).

24 O'Brien memo (NLI, MS 449, f. 3399); Duffy, *Four Years*, pp. 591–3; Irish Confederation minute books (RIA, MS 23/H/44, 3 May 1848, pp. 275–7).

25 Lord Clarendon to Sir George Grey, 27 Mar. 1848 (TNA, HO 45/2520 A); Seán McConville, *Irish Political Prisoners, 1848–1922: Theatres of War* (London, 2003), p. 26.

26 *Times*, 20 May 1848; Hugh Ross O'Loghlen to [George?] Bryan, [May 1848] (NLI, MS 3226/9); *Nation*, 27 May 1848.

27 Untitled handbill (TNA, PRO, 30/22/7C–6).

28 Mitchel, *Last Conquest*, p. 188; Dillon, *Mitchel*, I, p. 247; John O'Leary, *Recollections of Fenians and Fenianism* (2 vols, London, 1896), I, pp. 9–10; John Savage, *Fenian Heroes and Martyrs* (Boston, 1868), p. 47.

29 *Irish Felon*, 24 June 1848.

30 Mitchel, *Jail Journal*, pp. 1–4, 14.

31 *Times*, 29 May 1848, 14 Dec. 1853, 15 May 1848, 28 Apr. 1854, 23 Sept. 1858, 31 Aug. 1859; *Punch*, 8 Apr. 1848.

32 John O'Donovan to Daniel McCarthy, 2 June 1848 (NLI, MS 132); Dillon, *Mitchel*, I, p. 320; W. J. Lowe, 'The Chartists and the Irish Confederates: Lancashire, 1848', *Irish Historical Studies* XXIV: 94 (Nov., 1984), p. 179; *Nation*, 27 May, 17 June 1848.

Chapter 4: *In Exile, 1848–53*

1 John Mitchel, *Jail Journal, or Five Years in British Prisons* (enlarged edn with a preface by Arthur Griffith, Dublin, [1913]), pp. 39, 35, 96, 122.

2 Mitchel to Matilda Mitchel, 5 Mar. 1849 (PRONI, D/1078/M/4); Mitchel, *Jail Journal*, pp. 47–9.

3 Mitchel, *Jail Journal*, pp. 37, 58, 72–3.

4 Ibid., p. 60.

5 Ibid., pp. 80, 91–2.

6 Review of *The Purgatory of Suicides* in *Nation*, 8 Nov. 1845.

7 John Mitchel, *Apology for the British Government in Ireland* (Dublin, 1920), p. 3.

8 Mitchel, *Jail Journal*, pp. 86–7.

9 Ibid., pp. 20, 29, 128n.

10 *United Irishman*, 29 Apr. 1848, p. 186; Mitchel, *Jail Journal*, p. 20. For a fuller account of Mitchel's views see James Quinn, 'John Mitchel and the rejection of the nineteenth century', *Éire–Ireland* XXXVIII: 3–4 (fall/winter 2003), pp. 90–108.

11 *Citizen*, 15 July 1854.

12 Mitchel, *Jail Journal*, pp. 26, 27, 28.

13 Ibid., pp. 87, 376–7.

14 Mitchel to Matilda Mitchel, 5 Mar. 1849 (PRONI, D/1078/M/4); Mitchel, *Jail Journal*, pp. 96, 107, 112.

15 Mitchel, *Jail Journal*, pp. 149, 152.

16 Ibid., pp. 182–5, 195; Mitchel to Dillon, 9 Nov. 1850 (Bigger coll., Z314(5)-3).

17 Mitchel to O'Brien, June 1850 (NLI, MS 444/2696).

18 Martin to Meagher, 11 Apr. 1850 (T. J. Kiernan, *The Irish Exiles in Australia* (Melbourne, 1954), p. 80); Mitchel, *Jail Journal*, pp. 235–6.

19 Meagher to Sir Colman O'Loghlen, 27 Aug. 1851 (NLI, MS 3226/79).

20 Mitchel to O'Brien, June 1850 (NLI, MS 444/2696); Mitchel, *Jail Journal*, p. 246.

21 Martin's diary, 22 Sept. 1850 (PRONI, D/560/4, p. 2); Mitchel, *Jail Journal*, pp. 249, 282–5.

22 T. B. McManus to R. J. Tyler, 14 July 1851 (NLI, MS 6456/150).

23 O'Brien's journal, 15–16 Oct. 1851 (Richard Davis (ed.), '*To Solitude Consigned': The Tasmanian Journal of William Smith O'Brien* (Sydney, 1995), pp. 277–8).

24 Mitchel to Mary Thomson, 4 Oct. 1852 (William Dillon, *Life of John Mitchel* (2 vols, London, 1888), I, p. 339); Mitchel, *Jail Journal*, pp. 266–7.

25 Mitchel, *Jail Journal*, pp. 230–1, 263, 286, 245.

26 *Citizen*, 15 July 1854.

27 Mitchel, *Jail Journal*, pp. 124–5; *Citizen*, 11 Feb. 1853.

28 Mitchel to O'Brien, June 1850, 7 Sept. 1851 (NLI, MS 444, ff. 2696, 2794); Dillon, *Mitchel*, I, pp. 331, 340.

29 Mitchel, *Jail Journal*, pp. 278–9.

30 Mitchel to O'Doherty, 28 Aug. 1852 (NLI, MS 3226/89).

31 Mitchel to O'Brien, 19 Jan. 1852 (NLI, MS 444/2808); Mitchel to Mary Thomson, 4 Oct. 1852 (NLI, MS 329/1).

32 Mitchel, *Jail Journal*, pp. 300, 304, 309–11.

33 Ibid., pp. 318–49.

Chapter 5: *Liberty in America, 1853–4*

1 *New York Daily Times*, 30 Nov. 1853; Mitchel to Martin, 29 Oct. 1854 (Bigger coll., z314(5)).

2 William Dillon, *Life of John Mitchel* (2 vols, London, 1888), II, p. 50.

3 William D'Arcy, *The Fenian Movement in the United States, 1858–1886* (Washington, 1947), pp. 5–12.

4 John Mitchel, *Jail Journal, or Five Years in British Prisons* (enlarged edn with a preface by Arthur Griffith, Dublin, [1913]), pp. 378–9, 387.

5 Ibid., pp. 357–8; *Citizen*, 25 Mar. 1854.

6 *Citizen*, 15 July 1854.

7 *Citizen*, 15 July 1854.

8 C. G. Duffy, *Conversations with Carlyle* (London, 1892), p. 117; Maurice O'Connell, 'O'Connell, Young Ireland, and Negro slavery: an exercise in romantic nationalism', *Thought* LX: 253 (June 1989), pp. 132–3; Douglas C. Riach, 'Daniel O'Connell and American anti-slavery', *Irish Historical Studies* XX: 77 (Mar. 1976), pp. 3–27; *Citizen*, 4 Mar. 1854.

9 *Citizen*, 14 Jan. 1854.

10 *New York Daily Times*, 27 Jan., 3 Feb. 1854; *Citizen*, 28 Jan. 1854.

11 Mitchel to Kenyon, *c.* Nov. 1857 (Dillon, *Mitchel*, II, p. 106). On Carlyle's influence on Mitchel see Duffy, *Conversations with Carlyle*, p. 117.

12 *Citizen*, 23 Sept. 1854 (Mitchel's italics).

13 *Citizen*, 11, 18 Feb., 7 Oct., 25 Nov., 16 Dec. 1854.

14 *Citizen*, 28 Jan., 23 Sept., 11 Feb. 1854.

15 *New York Daily Times*, 4, 10, 12 Aug. 1853; *Citizen*, 19 Aug., 9 Sept. 1853.

16 'Journal', *Irish Citizen*, 11 Sept. 1869.

Chapter 6: *Southern Citizen, 1855–65*

1 'Journal', *Irish Citizen*, 23 Oct. 1869.

2 Mitchel to Mrs Williams, Bothwell, 24 July 1855 (NLI, MS 3226/108); 'Journal', *Irish Citizen*, 6 Nov. 1869.

3 'Journal', *Irish Citizen*, 20 Nov. 1869.

4   Mitchel to Adelaide Dillon, 22 Dec. 1859 (Bigger coll., Z 314(5)–4); 'Journal', *Irish Citizen*, 11 Dec. 1869; 'Tour of the cotton states', *Irishman*, 1 Feb. 1862; 'John Mitchel's daughter', *Irish Monthly* XIV (Mar. 1886), p. 139.

5   John Mitchel, *Apology for the British Government in Ireland* (Dublin, 1920), p. 4; *Irish Citizen*, 20 Nov. 1869.

6   *Irish Citizen*, 16 Oct. 1869; Mitchel to Mary Thomson, 26 Aug. 1854 (NLI, MS 329/4); Mitchel to Mary Thomson, 3 May 1847, and to his mother, 20 June 1857 (William Dillon, *Life of John Mitchel* (2 vols, London, 1888), II, pp. 96, 98).

7   Mitchel to his mother, 17 Feb. 1857, and to Henrietta Mitchel, 9 Jan. 1858 (Bigger coll., Z314(5)–2).

8   'Journal', *Irish Citizen*, 25 Dec. 1869; *Irishman*, 8 Sept. 1860; William Dillon, *Life of John Mitchel* (2 vols, London, 1888), II, p. 117; DeeGee Lester, 'John Mitchel's wilderness years in Tennessee', *Éire–Ireland* XXV: 2 (summer 1990), p. 12.

9   'Journal', *Irish Citizen*, 28 Aug. 1869.

10 'Cotton states', 21 Jan. 1858 (*Irishman*, 25 Jan. 1862).

11 'Journal', *Irish Citizen*, 9 July 1869.

12 'Journal', *Irish Citizen*, 18 Dec. 1869.

13 Mitchel to Matilda Mitchel, 10 Apr. 1859 (PRONI, D /1078/M/7).

14 *Mobile Advertiser*, quoted in Lester, 'John Mitchel's wilderness years in Tennessee', p. 12.

15 *New York Daily Times*, 7, 15 Oct. 1857.

16 'Martin's diary', July 1858 (PRONI, D/560/5, p. 136); Mitchel to Mrs Williams, Bothwell, 16 Feb. 1858 (NLI, MS 3226/133); Mitchel to Adelaide Dillon, 1 Apr. 1856 (Bigger coll., Z314(5)-4).

17 Mitchel to Mary Thomson, c. Dec. 1857 (Dillon, *Mitchel*, II, pp. 107–8).

18 'Cotton states', 6 Feb. 1858 (*Irishman*, 8 Mar. 1862).

19 'Journal', *Irish Citizen*, 25 Dec. 1869; see also David T. Gleeson, 'Parallel struggles: Irish republicanism in the American South, 1798–1876', *Éire–Ireland* XXXIV: 2 (summer 1999), p. 110.

20 'Cotton states', 21 Jan. 1858 (*Irishman*, 25 Jan. 1862).

21 *Irishman*, 15 Feb. 1862.

22 *Irishman*, 1 July 1865.

23 Mitchel to Dillon, 24 Oct. 1860 (Bigger coll., Z314(5)–3).

24 Mitchel to Dillon, 8 Jan. 1860 (Bigger coll., Z314(5)); 'Journal', *Irish Citizen*, 29 Jan. 1870.

25 Mitchel to Martin, 16 Dec. 1860 (Bigger coll., Z314(5)–1); 'Journal', *Irish Citizen*, 29 Jan. 1870.

26 R. V. Comerford, 'Conspiring brotherhoods and contending elites, 1857–63' in W. E. Vaughan (ed.), *A New History of Ireland*, v: *Ireland under the Union, I: 1801–70* (Oxford, 1989), pp. 427–8.

27 Mitchel to Henrietta Mitchel, 3 Nov. 1861 (Bigger coll., z314(5)–2, 16).

28 Notes by John Augustus O'Shea (Bigger coll., z314(1)); Jeffry D. Wert, *Gettysburg, Day 3* (London, 2001), p. 199.

29 'Journal', *Irish Citizen*, 11, 18, 25 June 1870.

30 Mitchel to Martin, 25 Feb. 1864 (Bigger coll., z314(5)–1); Joseph M. Hernon, jr, *Celts, Catholics and Copperheads: Ireland Views the American Civil War*(Ohio, 1968), p. 92.

31 *Nation*, 2 Jan. 1864.

32 Mitchel to William Mitchel, *c.* July 1864 (Dillon, *Mitchel*, II, p. 205); 'Journal', *Irish Citizen*, 4 June 1870.

33 'Journal', *Irish Citizen*, 9 July 1870.

34 'Journal', *Irish Citizen*, 16 July 1870.

35 'Journal', *Irish Citizen*, 9, 23 July 1870; *Irishman*, 1 July 1865.

36 Mitchel to Margaret Mitchel, 3 June 1865 (Dillon, *Mitchel*, II, p. 214); *New York Daily News*, 30 May, 4, 15, 18 June 1865.

37 *New York Daily News*, 3, 13 June 1865.

38 *Irish Citizen*, 3 Sept. 1870.

39 Dillon, *Mitchel*, II, p. 224; 'Journal', *Irish Citizen*, 30 July 1870.

40 'Journal', *Irish Citizen*, 13 Aug. 1870.

41 'Journal', *Irish Citizen*, 30 July 1870.

Chapter 7: *Fenians and Home Rule, 1865–75*

1 O'Mahony to Mitchel, 10 Nov. 1865 (Joseph Denieffe, *A Personal Narrative of the Irish Revolutionary Brotherhood*(Shannon, 1969), p. 201); Mitchel to Mary Thomson, 31 Jan. 1866 (William Dillon, *Life of John Mitchel* (2 vols, London, 1888), II, p. 235); Mitchel to Martin, 7 Dec. 1865 (Bigger coll., z314(5)–1).

2 Desmond Ryan, *The Fenian Chief: A Biography of James Stephens* (Dublin, 1967), pp. 111, 222; Denieffe, *Personal Narrative*, p. 220; *Nation*, 14 July 1866; Dillon, *Mitchel*, II, p. 244.

3 Mitchel to Mortimer Moynahan, 28 Jan. 1867 (William D'Arcy, *The Fenian Movement in the United States, 1858–1886* (Washington, 1947), p. 226); *Irish Citizen*, 18 Jan., 22 Feb. 1868.

4 *Irish Citizen*, 22, 29 Feb., 24 Apr. 1868.

5 Mitchel to Martin, 28 Mar. [1868?] and n.d. (Bigger coll., z314(5)–1); D'Arcy, *Fenian Movement*, p. 383n.

6   Mitchel to Martin, 24 Sept. 1871 (Bigger coll., Z314(5)–1); *Irish Citizen*, 20 Apr. 1872.

7   *Irish Citizen*, 5 Feb. 1870.

8   *Irish Citizen*, 3 Sept. 1870.

9   *Irish Citizen*, 25 Mar. 1871, 30 Mar., 13 Apr., 13 July 1872.

10 *Irish Citizen*, 4 Jan. 1868.

11 Mitchel to Dillon, 26 Mar. 1866 (Bigger coll., Z314(5)).

12 Mitchel to Mary Thomson, 24 Apr. 1854 (NLI, MS 329/3); 'Cotton states', 23, 29 Jan. 1858 (*Irishman*, 1, 15 Feb. 1862).

13 Mitchel to Matilda Mitchel, 5 Mar. 1849 (PRONI, D/1078/M/4); Mitchel, *Jail Journal*, p. 81.

14 Dillon, *Mitchel*, II, pp. 311–12; 'T. C. Luby's funeral oration for Mitchel (New York)' (NLI, MS 330, p. 24); *Irish American*, 28 Oct. 1865. My treatment of Mitchel's classical republicanism owes much to the interpretation in Patrick Maume, 'Young Ireland, Arthur Griffith, and republican ideology: the question of continuity', *Éire–Ireland* XXXIV: 2 (summer 1999), pp. 155–74.

15 D'Arcy, *Fenian Movement*, p. 391.

16 F. S. L. Lyons, *John Dillon: A Biography* (London, 1968), p. 16.

17 Dillon, *Mitchel*, II, pp 282–5; NAI, Chief Secretary's Office, Registered papers, 1874/1515, 1591; 1875/3657, 4131, 4193, 4285.

18 *Freeman's Journal*, 13 Mar. 1875.

19 Dillon, *Mitchel*, II, p. 289.

20 F. S. L. Lyons, *Charles Stewart Parnell* (London, 1977), p. 47; William O'Brien, *Recollections* (London, 1905), p. 112.

21 Dillon, *Mitchel*, II, p. 296.

Conclusion

1   *United Irishman*, 6 May 1848.

2   John Devoy, *Recollections of an Irish Rebel* (New York, 1929), pp. 9–10; Dominic Daly, *The Young Douglas Hyde* (Dublin, 1974), p. xviii; Eoin MacNeill (ed.), *An Ulsterman for Ireland* (Dublin, 1917), pp. v–vi; Amanda Sebestyen (ed.), *Prison Letters of Constance Markievicz* (London, 1987), p. 276; James Connolly, *Labour in Ireland* (Dublin, 1917), pp. 176–82.

3   P. H. Pearse, *From a Hermitage* (Dublin, 1915), p. 12; idem, *Ghosts* (Dublin, 1916), pp. 12, 20; idem, *The Sovereign People* (Dublin, 1916), pp. 17–18.

4   Cited in Brian Maye, *Arthur Griffith* (Dublin, 1997), p. 52; Mitchel, *Jail Journal, or Five Years in British Prisons* (enlarged edn, with a preface by Arthur Griffith (Dublin, [1913]), p. xiv; Arthur Griffith, *The Sinn Féin Policy* (Dublin,

1906), pp. 8–11; see also Richard Davis, *Arthur Griffith and Non-violent Sinn Féin* (Dublin, 1974), pp. 107, 127, 151, and Patrick Maume, *The Long Gestation: Irish Nationalist Life, 1891–1918* (Dublin, 1999), pp. 6, 49–53.

5   F. S. L. Lyons, *John Dillon: A Biography* (London, 1968), pp. 15–16, 22–3; Patrick Maume, 'Young Ireland, Arthur Griffith, and republican ideology: the question of continuity', *Éire–Ireland* XXXIV: 2 (summer 1999), p. 161; Michael Davitt, *Life and Progress in Australasia* (London, 1898), pp. 334–5.

6   Aodh de Blácam, *The Black North* (Dublin, 1938), p. 118.

Select Bibliography

Of Mitchel's own works, by far the most useful biographical source is his *Jail Journal, or Five Years in British Prisons*, first published in the *Citizen* (14 Jan. to 19 Aug. 1854); in book form (New York, 1854; 2nd edition, Glasgow, 1856); and an enlarged edition with a preface by Arthur Griffith (Dublin, 1913). Besides giving a detailed account of Mitchel's years in exile in Bermuda and Tasmania, it contains wide reflections on his political and social philosophy. 'A continuation of the jail journal', covering the years 1854 to 1866 was published in Mitchel's *Irish Citizen* newspaper (24 July 1869 to 10 Sept. 1870). Although not of the literary quality of the earlier journal, it is a valuable biographical source, especially for the American Civil War period. Of Mitchel's other published works, *The Last Conquest of Ireland (Perhaps)* (Dublin, 1861) contains some useful biographical material injected into a highly polemical account of Irish politics and society before and during the Great Famine.

The first biography of Mitchel was John B. Bannon, *Life of Mitchel* (Liverpool, 1882), a short, competent work, written by a Jesuit who acted as a Confederate agent in Ireland during the American Civil War, and who knew and admired Mitchel. The best biography of Mitchel is William Dillon, *Life of John Mitchel* (2 vols, London, 1888). In writing this sympathetic but not uncritical work, Dillon had the co-operation of Mitchel's family and access to their papers, and it contains long extracts from several letters which are now lost. Other biographies are P. A. Silliard, *Life of Mitchel* (Dublin, 1889); P. S. O'Hegarty, *John Mitchel: An Appreciation: With Some Account of Young Ireland* (Dublin, 1917); Louis J. Walsh, *John Mitchel* (Dublin, 1934); Niall Ó Domhnaill, *Beatha Sheáin Mistéil* (Dublin, 1937); and Séamas MacCall, *Irish Mitchel: A Biography* (London, 1938). All are admiring accounts written from a nationalist point of view. MacCall's is probably the best of these: it is well written, and apparently well researched, but lacks footnotes. Brendan Ó Cathaoir's pamphlet, *John Mitchel* (Dublin, 1978), is a short but insightful treatment.

Accounts by contemporaries that provide some interesting perspectives
on Mitchel include Charles Gavan Duffy, *Four Years of Irish History* (London,
1883) and *Young Ireland: A Fragment of Irish History* (London, 1880); Michael
Doheny, *The Felon's Track* (Dublin, 1918); and Richard Davis (ed.), *'To Solitude
Consigned': The Tasmanian Journal of William Smith O'Brien* (Sydney, 1995).

Some useful biographies of contemporaries are Rebecca O'Conner, *Jenny
Mitchel: Young Irelander: A Biography* (Dublin, 1988), a quirky but lively and well-
researched work, although unfortunately it is not footnoted; John N. Molony,
A Soul Came Into Ireland: Thomas Davis, 1814–1845 (Dublin, 1995); Helen
F. Mulvey, *Thomas Davis and Ireland: a biographical study* (Washington, 2003);
Brendan Ó Cathaoir, *John Blake Dillon: Young Irelander* (Dublin, 1990); Ellen
Shannon Mangan, *James Clarence Mangan* (Dublin, 1996); R. P. Davis, *William
Smith O'Brien: Ireland – 1848 – Tasmania* (Dublin, 1989); and Robert Sloan,
William Smith O'Brien and the Young Ireland Rebellion of 1848 (Dublin, 2000).

The following articles are useful: DeeGee Lester, 'John Mitchel's wilder-
ness years in Tennessee', *Éire–Ireland* XXV: 2 (summer 1990), pp. 7–13; Mary
Buckley, 'John Mitchel: Ulster and Irish nationality, 1842–48', *Studies* LXV
(spring 1976), pp. 30–44; John Newsinger, 'John Mitchel and Irish nationalism',
Literature and History VI (1980), pp. 182–200; Graham Davis, 'Making history:
John Mitchel and the Great Famine' in Paul Hyland and Neil Sammells (eds),
Irish Writing, Exile and Subversion (London, 1991), pp. 98–115; Gerry Kearns,
'"Educate that holy hatred": place, trauma and identity in the Irish nationalism
of John Mitchel', *Political Geography* XX: 7 (Sept. 2001), pp. 885–911; and James
Quinn, 'John Mitchel and the rejection of the nineteenth century', *Éire–
Ireland* XXXVIII: 3–4 (fall/winter 2003), pp. 90–108. Steven R. Knowlton makes an
unconvincing case for Mitchel as a champion of individual liberty in 'The
politics of John Mitchel: a reappraisal', *Éire–Ireland* XXII: 2 (summer 1987), pp.
38–55. Robert Mahony examines the influence of the Trinitarian controversy
of the 1820s on Mitchel's thought in '"New Light" Ulster Presbyterianism and
the nationalist rhetoric of John Mitchel' in Laurence M. Geary (ed.), *Rebellion
and Remembrance in Modern Ireland* (Dublin, 2001), pp. 148–58.

On the background to Mitchel's political career in the 1840s see Kevin
B. Nowlan, *The Politics of Repeal* (London, 1965); Richard Davis, *The Young
Ireland Movement* (Dublin, 1987); Denis Gwynn, *Young Ireland and 1848* (Cork,
1949); and the relevant chapters in W. E. Vaughan (ed.), *A New History of
Ireland*, V: *Ireland under the Union, I: 1801–70* (Oxford, 1989). On the Famine
see especially Cormac Ó Gráda, *Black '47 and Beyond: The Great Irish Famine
in History, Economy, and Memory* (Princeton, 1999); Peter Gray, *Famine, Land
and Politics: British Government and Irish Society, 1843–50* (Dublin, 1999); and

James S. Donnelly, jr, *The Great Irish Potato Famine* (Stroud, 2002). For
Mitchel's years in exile the most useful works are T. J. Kiernan, *The Irish Exiles
in Australia* (Melbourne, 1954); Blanche M. Touhill, *William Smith O'Brien and
His Irish Revolutionary Companions in Penal Exile* (Columbia and London,
1981); and Thomas Keneally, *The Great Shame* (London, 1998). The sources
on Mitchel in America are rather fragmentary, but see David T. Gleeson,
'Parallel struggles: Irish republicanism in the American South, 1798–1876',
Éire–Ireland XXXIV: 2 (summer 1999), 97–116; and William D'Arcy, *The Fenian
Movement in the United States 1858–1886* (Washington, 1947).

INDEX